THE WORLD'S MOST
**SENSATIONAL
SCANDALS**

THE WORLD'S MOST
SENSATIONAL SCANDALS

BY
NIGEL BLUNDELL

SUNBURST BOOKS

PHOTOGRAPHY CREDITS

Express Newspapers Plc: 46, 72, 78, 83, 132, 157, 168.
Evening Standard: 39.
Associated Press: 103.
Camera Press: 110.
Alan Grisbrook: 118.
Reuters: 126.
Geoffrey Giuliano: 141.
Penthouse Magazine: 176.
Rex Pictures: 178.
Press Association: 186.
Copyright unknown: 54, 62, 64, 66, 70, 74, 151.

Copyright text © Nigel Blundell 1995
Copyright design © Sunburst Books 1995

This edition published 1995 by Sunburst Books, Deacon House,
65 Old Church Street, London SW3 5BS

The right of Nigel Blundell to be identified as the author of this work has been asserted in
accordance with the Copyright, Designs and Patents Act 1988.

ISBN 1 85778 064 7

Printed and bound in the United Kingdom

Contents

Introduction

Why do they do it? It's the question asked every time a scandal breaks.

Why do people in power risk everything for greed, for a brief fling or for a mere sensation of the moment?

Profumo to Presley, Princess Margaret to Princess Michael – all have been involved in public scandal. *The World's Most Sensational Scandals* documents how the people to whom image is everything manage to drag their own names through the dirt.

Blunt, Profumo, Watergate ... these scandals not only make fascinating reading, but have also changed the course of history.

SOUTH SEA BUBBLE

Like all the juiciest financial scandals, the South Sea Bubble relied on two vital characteristics among investors: greed and ignorance.

It was a lethal combination which ruined a massive cross-section of British society from lords to labourers. None of them really understood how credit worked. But at the time they didn't care. They didn't so much jump on to the bandwagon; more like fitted it with a turbo-charger.

The South Sea Company was formed in 1711 with the then perfectly acceptable aim of shipping black slaves from Africa to South America. A concession to trade had been wheedled out of the French King Louis XIV (who had himself been given that right by the occupying Spanish). The agreement was instantly hailed as a milestone in improved Anglo-French relations.

For the company, however, the first few years proved grim. For a start, the available concessions were restrictive and hardly profitable. The slaves died by the hundred in appalling conditions during the voyage across the South Atlantic. And pirates made matters worse by flooding the market with slaves at rock-bottom prices. Even the announcement that the king himself, George I, had become the company's governor failed to lift lacklustre balance sheets.

The turn-around came when a conniving director of the South Sea Company, John Blunt, seized upon the idea of credit management, a system already being exploited well in France by the Scottish financier, John Law. Law's theory was that governments should issue paper money through national banks instead of gold. The paper notes had to carry the pledge that they could be exchanged for gold at any time – otherwise the financial community would have no confidence in them. But once confidence was established, a government could simply print more notes whenever it was short of cash.

It seemed too good to be true, which of course it was. Today we know that such a policy is doomed to end in rampant inflation. But at the time the likes of John Law and John Blunt saw their schemes as economic miracles which could not fail.

Blunt persuaded his fellow directors at the South Sea Company to embark on a business plan in which they would take total responsibility for England's National Debt (the £50 million the government had borrowed from its own citizens). They would even pay £8 million for the privilege.

The plan went like this. Anyone with, say, £10,000 worth of government bonds could redeem them at the usual, modest rate of interest, or he could choose to re-invest in South Sea stock with its promise of fabulous rewards. Each company share would be launched on the market for £100, and so the £10,000 investor would receive 100 spanking new printed shares.

But what if the publicity and excitement generated by this imaginative new venture was such that there was a huge demand? Shares would then naturally rise in price – perhaps even double to £200 apiece. The next £10,000 investor to come along would need only 50 shares from the company, leaving another 50 to sell to someone else. The instant profit for the company would amount to £10,000. The key was to keep the sale price of the shares rising so that there were always new investors ready to jump on board.

The idea went before Parliament on 22 January 1720 and, despite noisy objections from the Bank of England which saw its own role being eroded, it was approved by a majority of four votes. Supporters believed the deal was good for the country because the government would pay the company only 4% interest on loans rather than the usual 5%. Within a quarter of a century, it was claimed, the National Debt slate would be wiped clean and England would once again be able to trade with the world unfettered by the financial millstone around her neck.

At first it seemed these supporters were right. The share price quickly rocketed to £400 before a few jubilant, early profit-takers damped it down to a steady £330.

Within a matter of weeks widows and pensioners were retrieving their meagre life-savings from beneath mattresses to plough into the South Sea Company. Farm workers and fishermen rushed to buy their stake before the price spiralled again. The landed gentry poured in every last penny they could find. Some even re-mortgaged their homes or borrowed from more circumspect friends to increase their exposure to this amazing new, no-risk wonder-company.

The frenzy persisted even when three months after the launch Blunt revealed another 20,000 shares were up for grabs. This was an illegal move as Parliament had decreed the only shares that could be sold were remainders left after government creditors and pensioners had received their full allocation.

It didn't seem to matter. The new stock sold for £300 per share and a further 10,000 floated later in the month went for £400. Many people took their lead from the king who had let it be known of his own £20,000 investment. George sold his stake for a handsome £86,000 profit early on and was so pleased with John Blunt's performance that he awarded him a knighthood.

Incredibly, none of the money that came in was reinvested by the South Sea Company. No one stopped to think that it should be put to work – making things or providing services for consumers. Directors of the company wallowed complacently in the belief that if they needed more money, they just printed more shares.

Before 1720 was out, a host of other entrepreneurs were taking a slice of the action with their own hastily-formed companies. Most of these were illegal because they were trading without a royal charter. However, both the authorities and the general public were too busy getting rich quick to care. Hence anyone could buy shares in pirate-proof ships, cleaner lavatories or wheels which produced perpetual motion. Investors could get into the jackasses-from-

Spain import business or silkworm production in Chelsea.

One sincere-looking entrepreneur even sold shares in a company whose declared aim was 'carrying on an undertaking of great advantage but no one to know what it is'. He promised an annual return of £50 on every £1 invested and on his first day pocketed £2,000 from excited punters. The man vanished that evening, his undertaking of great advantage complete.

By August 1720 the South Sea Company had taken more than £8 million from its shareholders. Because many had bought under hire-purchase type agreements there was £60 million worth of payments still to come in. By now some of the new 'bubble' companies were starting to go bust – a factor that further slowed the flow of funds into Blunt's coffers.

The mood was imperceptibly changing, but Blunt failed to see it. He ordered the prosecution of four large rival companies which, he alleged, were trading without a royal charter. The courts backed Blunt and the companies' stock became worthless. Rarely in the field of great financial disasters has anyone misjudged the might of market forces so badly.

Investors in the four bankrupt companies decided to solve their personal financial problems by selling their best assets – South Sea Company Shares. Suddenly, instead of everyone wanting to buy, numerous big 'players' wanted to sell. Word spread and smaller investors picked up the vibes. Confidence, the factor that drives any credit economy, was taking a massive nose dive.

Within days South Sea shares were in free-fall. Their value was reduced from £900 apiece to £190, and thousands of people stared ruin in the face. The Duke of Chandos saw £300,000 disappear almost overnight and poets such as Alexander Pope and Matthew Prior also saw their life-savings trickle away.

MPs and the public were outraged. They felt swindled and they demanded a scapegoat. Blunt was the obvious option and he was hauled before a parliamentary committee to be told his personal £185,000 fortune would be reduced to £1,000. Another director with a £40,000 nest egg was shown the door with only £31 to his name. It did little to assuage public anger. At one point the king even considered bringing over his German troops from Hanover in case of a riot.

Yet, for all its crazy theories, the South Sea Bubble did not destroy the English economy. A boom in overseas trade helped many of the worst-hit businessmen re-build their mini-empires. And, of course, those who sold their shares at the right time had become very rich indeed.

Rather than robbing the nation's wealth, the 'Bubble' is now best remembered for simply shifting it around!

SCOTLAND YARD BRIBERY

In the 1870s Scotland Yard found itself dealing with an upsurge in swindlers and conmen. Pressure on the police to catch these scoundrels was intense, not least because their gullible victims tended to be the rich and influential in society. Fleecing the wealthy was easy money for the skilled operator.

They didn't come any more skilful than Harry Benson, a man whose eye for the main chance and confidence in his own smooth-talking ability marked him out as the prince of charlatans. Benson, son of a respectable Jewish merchant, portrayed himself as a member of the European nobility. His ability to speak several languages fluently impressed his acquaintances and he carried off his image as an educated gentleman with panache.

That is not to say he didn't make mistakes. At the end of the Franco–Prussian war of 1870-71 he turned up in London calling himself the Comte de Montague, Mayor of Chateaudun, and persuaded the Lord Mayor of London to hand him £1,000 towards the relief of war refugees. Hardly had he pocketed the cash than his forged receipt was spotted and he spent an uncomfortable year in prison.

It was an experience so loathsome to him that he tried to commit suicide in the most horrific manner, attempting to incinerate himself on his prison mattress. The flames left him half-crippled and restricted him to walking only with the aid of crutches.

On leaving prison, Benson advertised his services as a multilingual secretary and was approached by a man called William Kurr who made his living through gambling swindles. Kurr's usual method was to place bets for clients at a race meeting and then vanish with the proceeds of any big win. It was a primitive technique, but effective enough.

The two men quickly got the measure of each other and soon Benson was persuading Kurr to try more sophisticated scams. They began publishing a newspaper called *Le Sport*, which comprised mainly British racing articles translated into French. It was delivered free to selected French aristocrats with a keen interest in the turf.

Those who bothered to scan its pages read how a professional British punter called Mr G.H. Yonge had such an incredibly successful track record that many bookies cut the odds whenever they did business with him. Funnily enough, some of the aristocrats soon began receiving letters from Mr Yonge in which they were asked to act as his agent in laying bets. He could not, he explained, trade in his real name because bookmakers wouldn't give him decent odds.

All his agents had to do was receive a cheque, forward it to a certain bookmaker in their own own name and return the winnings to Mr Yonge. In return the agent would receive a 5% commission.

One wealthy Frenchwoman, the Comtesse de Goncourt, found this a particularly agreeable arrangement. She would mail Mr Yonge's cheque for several hundred pounds, receive back thousands in winnings and pocket £50 or so commission for herself. After a few trial runs she became so convinced that Yonge was a gambling genius that she asked him if he would mind very much investing £10,000 of her own money as he saw fit.

Unfortunately, the Comtesse did not cotton on to the simple truth that Yonge's 'bookmaker' was, like Yonge himself, just another of Benson's aliases. She never saw her £10,000 again.

Into this cauldron of deceit and doubletalk stepped a handful of detectives from Scotland Yard. Their stock in trade was to hobnob with 'narks', usually petty criminals who kept themselves out of jail by passing on useful criminal intelligence. The use of informers was, and remains, a vital part of police work. However, as any detective knows, there can be a fine line between professional agreements and corruption.

The taking of bribes was much more of a temptation to an officer of Victorian England (who earned a meagre £5 6s. 2d. a year) than to his present day colleagues. So when a Chief Inspector John Meiklejohn was offered cash presents by one William Kurr in return for dropping investigations into Kurr's criminal dealings, he readily accepted.

The web of corruption soon widened. A police friend of Meiklejohn's, Chief Inspector Nathaniel Druscovich, privately admitted that he had money worries. Meiklejohn introduced him to a 'business-man' who would help and soon the cheerful face of

Harry Benson was handing over a £60 'loan' to Druscovich. All he wanted in return, he said, was a little advance warning of any plan Scotland Yard might have to arrest him. The deal was struck then and there and soon a third detective, Chief Inspector William Palmer, was brought onto Benson's payroll.

Not long after the corrupt circle was in place, Meiklejohn delivered a warning to Benson that detectives were snapping at his heels. A Chief Inspector Clarke had been assigned to close down bogus bookmakers and he was very interested in the firm of Gardner & Co, the front company used by Kurr, Benson and their cohorts.

One of those cohorts was a swindler called Walters, whom Clarke had encountered while he was in the process of smashing another gang. With impressive nerve, Benson (using his Yonge alias) wrote to the officer inviting him to visit his palatial country home at Shanklin, on the Isle of Wight. He explained that he had some useful criminal intelligence but that he couldn't get up to London because he was crippled. Intrigued, and keen for a chance to mix with the upper classes, Clarke headed for Shanklin.

There Clarke was informed by Mr Yonge that Walters had been boasting of success in bribing him. Worse, that he still had a letter penned by the Chief Inspector which proved the allegation. Clarke had once written to Walters and he now acknowledged that his words were open to misinterpretation.

It seems this whole episode was cooked up by

Benson to try to warn Clarke off. If so, it failed. The officer reported to his superiors that Yonge was probably a crook and Benson's next move signalled the beginning of the end of his swindling career.

He contacted the Comtesse de Goncourt with the offer of a unique investment opportunity. She swallowed his line and instructed her solicitor to convert a number of assets into ready cash. However, the solicitor was suspicious. He contacted Scotland Yard to make sure this Mr Yonge had no criminal record. The message was intercepted by Druscovich, who immediately warned Benson of his imminent peril.

Benson, Kurr and the rest of the gang pulled £16,000 in cash out of a Bank of England account and headed for Scotland in the hope their trail would go cold. It didn't. Druscovich was dispatched to arrest them, but before he did, he sent a telegram warning Benson that he was on his way. Soon after this he and the other two 'bent' officers received £500 apiece for their trouble.

Senior detectives at Scotland Yard were by now growing frustrated and puzzled at their inability to nail the Benson gang. At first the thought that men within their own ranks had been 'nobbled' did not even occur to them. Even when Meiklejohn was spotted hobnobbing with the crooks at their hideaway in Bridge of Allan, Scotland, he talked himself out of the hole, claiming he didn't realise they were scoundrels.

As the heat increased, Benson fled to Holland.

There he tried to pass a £100 Bank of Clydesdale note, which Scotland Yard knew was one of a batch he had withdrawn some weeks earlier. They had already alerted Dutch police to the possibility that Benson (or one of his aliases) would turn up on their doorstep and now the Dutch moved in to make an arrest. Druscovich was briefed to bring the suspect home and he realised he could do his crooked benefactors no more favours.

The rest of the gang was duly rounded up, tried and sentenced. Benson got fifteen years and Kurr got ten years. Within hours of their arrival at London's Millbank prison they demanded to see the governor and spilt the beans on the network of corruption they had established within the very heart of Scotland Yard.

Druscovich, Meiklejohn and Palmer were later convicted of conspiring to pervert the course of justice and all were sentenced to the maximum two years hard labour. Clarke was acquitted and, although forcibly retired, was permitted to keep his police pension.

When the jailed officers were released, Meiklejohn set himself up in business as a private eye, while Palmer used his life-savings to open a pub. Little is known of Druscovich's fate; he appears to have deliberately kept a low profile.

Benson and Kerr both got time off their sentences for good behaviour. They teamed up again, this time as mining company consultants in the US, and soon the hapless European public was being offered shares in mines that didn't exist. Benson was again arrested and served two years in a Swiss prison.

His last great con was in Mexico, selling bogus tickets for the concerts of the celebrated US singer, Adelina Patti. On his return to the US, he received yet another prison sentence – this time in the infamous Tombs. He couldn't face the prospect and committed suicide by breaking his back in a leap off a 40 ft prison balcony.

CLEVELAND STREET
SCANDAL

When cash disappeared from a desk at the General Post Office, St Martin's-Le-Grand, City of London, in July 1889, telegraph messenger boys were the obvious suspects. Several were questioned by police and one, Charles Swinscow, was found to be carrying the unusually large amount of eighteen shillings. It was unthinkable that this fifteen-year-old boy could have saved up the money from his meagre pay packet. There was little doubt that he was the thief...

Until, that is, Swinscow gave his explanation. He claimed he had got the money by doing 'private work' for a gentleman called Charles Hammond of No.19, Cleveland Street. He had been introduced to Hammond by a fellow post office worker called Henry Newlove. With some embarrassment, Swinscow went on to admit that Newlove, a boy his own age, had seduced him in the basement toilets at the Post Office.

Later he had gone with Newlove to the Cleveland Street address where the pimp Hammond had invited him to perform similar acts for homosexual clients. Swinscow told how he'd gone to bed with a gentleman who 'put his person between my legs and an emission took place'. He was given half a sovereign which he handed to Hammond. His own cut was four shillings.

The names of other boys in the sex-for-sale scandal were soon wheedled out of Swinscow. Seventeen-year-olds George Wright and Charles Thickbroom were interviewed and they told how they had submitted to Newlove's urges in the basement toilets before being introduced at Cleveland Street. Both had willingly become rent boys at the four-shillings-per-client going rate.

It seemed police had stumbled across a vice den in the heart of London's Soho district. Newlove admitted that the allegations were true and was allowed bail. First thing the following day he was hammering on the door of No. 19 warning Hammond that the game was up. His mentor and employer thanked him profusely and immediately packed his bags to begin a new life in France. Another homosexual at the address, George Veck, who used the guise of a clergyman, also moved out.

The following day when officers arrived with an arrest warrant they found the address empty. But while Hammond had the financial means to get away, Newlove had no such luxury. As he was marched to the cells facing a charge of criminal conspiracy, the injustice of the whole business suddenly struck him.

It was hard, he told the policemen, that he should be thrown in prison while 'men in high positions' should be allowed to walk free. The officers were intrigued. What did he mean? The reply was dynamite.

"Lord Arthur Somerset goes regularly to the house

in Cleveland Street," blurted out Newlove. "So does the Earl of Euston and Colonel Jervois."

Lord Somerset, a major in the Royal Horse Guards and superintendent at the stables of Queen Victoria's son, the Prince of Wales, was a society figure of enormous repute. To link his name with the grubby goings on at Cleveland Street would, police knew, be the end of his reputation and career.

At first they treated Newlove's claim with healthy scepticism. However, when the rent boys Swinscow and Thickbroom positively (and separately) identified the peer as the man who had climbed into bed with them, it was clear a major society scandal was emerging.

When Somerset, known to his acquaintances as Podge, heard the news he arranged a four-month holiday and vanished to the Continent. His family fought hard to keep a lid on the whole affair. They had already experienced the shame of sexual misdemeanour. Podge's elder brother Henry had lost a wife who could not accept his sexual appetite for young men.

It did not take long for the press to sniff out the story. Veck was apprehended, and as he and Newlove awaited their trial, the *Pall Mall Gazette* ran a short story condemning the 'disgraceful nature' of the charges against them. It questioned whether 'two noble lords and other notable persons in society' were going to walk away from the affair scot free.

Behind the scenes there was further intrigue. Lord Somerset's solicitor, Arthur Newton, is said to have arranged a meeting with the Director of Public Prosecutions, Sir Augustus Stephenson, to discuss the case. Newton pointed out that if his lordship was prosecuted the names of other gentlemen would inevitably get dragged in. He mentioned rumours of one particular visitor to Cleveland Street, a man called Eddy, otherwise known as the Duke of Clarence, the son of the Prince of Wales.

Newton's intervention was timely because the evidence against his client was piling up. A teenager called Algernon Allies signed affidavits saying Lord Somerset, whom he knew as Mr Brown, had behaved indecently towards him. That was enough for the DPP. He wrote to the Attorney General, the government's top law officer, stating: "The prosecution wishes to avoid putting any witness in the box who refers to 'Mr Brown'."

It was therefore unsurprising that the case against Veck and Newlove was dealt with inside 30 minutes. Both men pleaded guilty and both were rewarded with light sentences: nine months hard labour for Veck and four months for Newlove. The Establishment breathed a collective sigh of relief. There had been no need to mention the involvement of the English aristocracy.

But as the lawyers streamed out of Bow Street court on the morning of 18 September 1889, any celebration of the whitewash was premature. Newspaper editors had no intention of letting the matter die and there were several who rightly saw themselves as a check against the abuses of the rich and powerful.

On 16 November, Ernest Parke of *The North London Press* was first to break ranks, naming both the Earl of Euston and Lord Somerset as clients at Cleveland Street. He also referred to a 'far more distinguished and more highly-placed personage (being) inculpated in these disgusting crimes'. Parke's account was a brave attempt to get at the truth but was inaccurate in one vital respect. He had accused the Earl of Euston of running off to Peru when in fact the earl had done no such thing.

Although several witnesses swore on oath that they had seen Euston wandering in and out of the brothel (one even told how the peer took him to bed), it was not enough for the jury. They accepted the plaintiff's account of how he had blundered in to the house expecting to see naked girls appearing in classic Greek poses. A doorman had explained to him the sexual services that were on offer, to which Euston apparently replied: "You infernal scoundrel, if you don't let me out I'll knock you down."

Parke was himself charged with 'libel without justification' and was sentenced to a year in prison without hard labour, a sentence widely seen as lenient by the standards of the times. Yet that was not the end of the drama. In December 1889 Lord Somerset's adviser, the solicitor Newton, was accused of interfering with witnesses. It was alleged he had sought an interview with Algy Allies and had tried to persuade three of the telegraph boys interviewed by police to spend some time abroad.

Later, he claimed, this was because Somerset's father, the Duke of Beaufort, wanted to meet the boys to see if they had been intimidated by police. Newton acknowledged that he was technically guilty of an offence but insisted that his motives were honourable. He escaped with only a six week sentence, though later he would spend more than two years in prison – the result of his forging a 'confession' by the infamous murderer Crippen.

And what of the other main players in the scandal?

Lord Somerset spent the rest of his days living abroad, stubbornly ignoring the view of family solicitors that he had a good chance of clearing his name. He died in the south of France in 1926.

Euston successfully shrugged off the Cleveland Street stigma, rising to become a senior Freemason and later aide-de-camp to King Edward VII. He succumbed to an attack of dropsy in 1912.

Hammond, the pimp in charge of the brothel, eventually settled in the USA and was never brought to trial.

As for the crusading editor, Ernest Parke, he found himself forgiven by the Establishment and ended up on retirement as a Justice of the Peace.

DREYFUS CASE

It started out as a straightforward case of espionage. Captain Alfred Dreyfus was convicted of spying for Germany against his homeland, France. He was stripped of his army rank and dispatched to Devil's Island as punishment.

However, suspicions that the disgraced Dreyfus was a 'fall guy' for the state soon rent the country in two. As months and years passed by, the aggrieved left-wing, feeling the evidence against Dreyfus was fabricated and that the reason for his victimisation was merely because he was Jewish, fermented into a frenzy.

The more vocal the support for Dreyfus, the more determined the right-wing government became to establish his guilt. The conflict between the two sides engulfed the entire country. Finally, top-ranking army officials were exposed as liars, Dreyfus was belatedly cleared and France was left looking ridiculous in the eyes of the world.

Born in 1859, Dreyfus came from a wealthy Jewish family which abandoned its home in Alsace when the Germans took control of the region. On the face of it, he seemed unlikely material for a spy.

Yet in September 1894, when an unsigned handwritten memo was fished from the bin of Colonel Max von Schwarzkoppen, the German military representative in Paris, it became obvious a French officer was spying and that man appeared to be Dreyfus.

The outspoken Dreyfus had already come to the attention of his superiors for his criticism of high-ranking army officers. It was also a time when anti-Semitism was rife throughout France.

Three men, Major Hubert-Joseph Henry, Colonel Jean-Conrad Sandherr and Major Du Paty de Calm, colluded in the arrest of Dreyfus. After comparing his writing to that on the illicit document, they decided he was guilty.

France was baying for blood when the trial of Dreyfus got underway in December 1894, having feasted on rumours and lies expounded by the French press. The hearing was held in secret, despite vigorous protests by Dreyfus's lawyer who wanted an open court.

Although the evidence against him was flimsy, Dreyfus was convicted as a traitor within three days. His penalty was deportation. Before that came the ritual humiliation of having his badges ripped from his uniform and his sword snapped in two. He was sent to Devil's Island, French Guiana, to endure years of solitary confinement and where, at night, he was shackled to his bed with iron chains.

There he might have remained had it not been for the intervention of Major Marie-Georges Picquart who replaced Sandherr in charge of scouring the nation for spies. From the same bin as the note that damned Dreyfus came a torn-up postcard bearing a cryptic message and addressed to a Major Marie-Chalres-Ferdinand Walsin-Esterhazy. The finger of guilt suddenly pointed towards him.

Esterhazy was already known for his overt curiosity about army secrets. Further, he was a long-time friend of Major Henry. When Picquart matched Esterhazy's handwriting to that on the original note, he knew a grave miscarriage of justice had been done.

Yet when he presented his findings to his superior, General Boisdeffre, he was told to keep the two cases separate. In other words, abandon Dreyfus and his only hope of freedom.

Picquart was appalled. His reward for his honesty and integrity was a hazardous posting in Tunisia where he was likely to die. He survived the conflict there, however, and continued to lobby on behalf of Dreyfus even though it cost him his career.

Now a radical newspaper took up the cause. Unconvinced by a court martial at which Esterhazy was cleared, *L'Aurore* published an open letter to the President in 1898 by the novelist Emile Zola, catchily titled *J'Accuse*. It denounced the government for its role in the scandalous Dreyfus affair in strong terms.

The government was left in a quandary. It could not allow Zola to escape punishment for his wide-ranging criticism. Yet neither did it want the Dreyfus case picked over in public again.

There was little option but to prosecute Zola, and he was charged over his claims that Esterhazy's acquittal was bogus. The writer was found guilty, fined and sentenced to a year behind bars.

Now claims and counter claims were flying around the country. Mobs supporting each side rioted and fought on the streets. Those opposing Dreyfus were still in the majority. His supporters were regarded by many as revolutionary left-wingers. Still, the questions over the case would not go away.

It was announced that Dreyfus' guilt had been proved by three letters which had just come to light. Immediately, it was declared these letters were forgeries. This was not only proved true but Henry confessed to being the author of the fraud. After he was arrested, Henry cut his own throat in jail.

In 1899 a new president gave the go-ahead for a retrial. Henry was dead, Boisdeffre had resigned and Paty de Calm was in prison for forging documents in the case. Still, Dreyfus was convicted of treason and sentenced to ten years in prison. It was then the man whose persecution created such mayhem in France suffered a nervous breakdown. Despite his better judgement, he agreed to a pardon for a crime he did not commit, making him a free man in September 1899.

Controversy raged on. The Dreyfus supporters, hated by the establishment, refused to be silenced. Zola, who had returned to France from exile at the news of a retrial, was found dead of carbon monoxide poisoning with his wife Alexandrine in their Paris home in 1902. It seemed their chimney had been deliberately blocked, probably by members of the anti-Dreyfus camp.

It wasn't until 1906 that a fresh inquiry announced there wasn't a shred of evidence against Dreyfus. In June that same year the French republic tried to make amends for the hardship it had inflicted on the innocent Dreyfus. Troops were assembled, just as they had been eleven years previously when he was drummed out of the army. This time General Guillain pinned a cross on Major Dreyfus' coats and elevated him to a Knight of the Legion of Honour.

Dreyfus stayed in the army just a year before resigning. Still the scandal refused to die. In June 1908 Dreyfus was at a ceremony in honour of his defender Zola when two shots were fired. He was slightly hurt. At the other end of a smoking revolver was journalist Sosthene Gregory, 65, who believed he had been striking a blow against 'Dreyfusism'. Ironically, Gregory was saved from the wrath of the crowd by Mathieu Dreyfus, loyal brother of Alfred, who had spent years campaigning for him.

Dreyfus himself returned to active service during World War I. He died on 13 July 1935, aged 75, just as anti-Semitism was poised to strike through the heart of Europe again – in the form of Nazism.

SALVADOR DALI

Some days, just for fun, Salvador Dali would sign hundreds upon hundreds of pieces of blank paper and distribute them to anyone he happened to meet. The result was a dream come true for art forgers; a licence to represent their work as that of the greatest surrealist painter of the 20th century. Lithographs carrying a genuine Dali signature flooded the market throughout the 1970s. The forgeries sold for hundreds of millions of dollars, scandalising the art world and poking fun at its pomposity.

Dali merely basked in all the attention. "No one would worry if I were a mediocre painter," he would observe, twitching his trademark waxed moustache. "All the great painters have been falsified." It was a classic Dali-ism. He relished every opportunity to shock, to outrage, and to undermine society's cherished values. Indeed, as he loved to point out to horrified art critics, his work came down to one principal philosophy – he was in it for the money.

There was little need to promote his talents because the 'Divine Dali' as he called himself was a superb self-publicist. "Every morning upon awakening," he would muse, "I experience a supreme pleasure: that of being Salvador Dali, and I ask myself, wonder-struck, what prodigious thing will he do today."

One of Dali's other great pleasures was to succeed in bamboozling the media and any art critic who tried to read symbolism into his work. During his first trip to the US (financed by Picasso) Dali welcomed reporters aboard the ship and immediately offered to show them his latest work; a nude study of his future wife, Gala Dimitrovna Diaharoff. His audience was impressed. But what was that on her shoulder? Surely some lamb chops. Was Dali trying to somehow contrast the beauty of the female form with the innate ugliness of the human psyche, the desire to kill other living things? Apparently not.

Dali explained: "It is very simple. I love Gala and I love lamb chops. Here they are together. Perfect harmony."

A little later he arrived at a New York lecture hall dressed from head to toe in a deep sea diving suit. It was, he said, the ideal garb for diving into the depths of the subconscious. It was not, however, the ideal garb in which to deliver lectures. Dali was lucky to escape suffocation after he forgot to equip himself with an air pump.

It was this 'in-your-face' laugh-a-minute attitude to the art establishment that made him so unpopular with many other Surrealists, as well as conservative sections of society.

So, when his Surrealist colleagues came out in favour of Communism, Dali espoused the Spanish royal family. When they spoke of the need for a simple, poverty stricken life to explore new art forms, he bragged about his desire for hard cash. And when they pompously announced that avante-garde experiments were the path to artistic integrity, Dali insisted he was just a good old-fashioned painter.

As he put it in his 1976 autobiography, *The Unspeakable Confessions of Salvador Dali*, "The clown is not I, but rather our monstrously cynical and so naively unconscious society that plays at the game of being serious, the better to hide its own madness. For I – I can never repeat it enough – am not mad."

Those who met Dali were not always reassured by such pronouncements. Wasn't this the man seen carrying a 5 ft tall purple model of Bugs Bunny through New York City claiming it was the most frightening animal in the world and that he intended to cover it with mayonnaise to make it a piece of object d'art? Wasn't this the same Dali who once invited a reporter into his garden on Spain's Costa Brava, pointed at a tree with two armchairs stuck in the branches and suggested they should climb up so that they could be more comfortable?

And hadn't he once confessed that he regularly spat on a portrait of his mother because it gave him so much pleasure? Madness is a difficult concept to define and Dali delighted in blurring the edge of sanity.

Even his birth was something of an unusual event because Dali stubbornly disputed the date it happened. Not the date he emerged from his mother's womb – he was satisfied with the records showing 11 May 1904 – but the date he became a living entity in his own right. Dali always insisted that he began an independent awareness while still a seven-month foetus. "It was warm, it was soft, it was silent, it was paradise," he would claim later.

As a child, Salvador Felipe Jacinto Dali decided early that he wanted to become a professional artist. By the age of ten he had produced his first two oils: *Helen of Troy* and *Joseph Greeting His Brethren*. He would sometimes search for inspiration by squatting in a tub in the laundry room.

At seventeen, he began a course at the Madrid-based San Fernando Academy of Fine Arts but found himself regularly at odds with the authorities. He was first suspended for twelve months for inciting a riot against the appointment of an 'unworthy' professor and in 1926 was booted out completely over allegations that he was a revolutionary sympathiser.

Free to pursue his own outrageous ideas, Dali now entered one of the most productive periods of his life. *The Great Masturbator* (1929) was typical of the obsession he had for including insects in his paintings; it showed a large pink head with long eyelashes, a bulbous nose resting on the ground and, in place of a mouth, a rotting grasshopper covered in ants.

Another work *The Persistence of Memory* (1931) is still regarded as Surrealism at its best. It shows wristwatches with their straps draped over a collection of unrelated objects, among them a withered tree. Woe betide any critic attempting a consideration of Dali's analysis of the painting. The watches, he said, were "nothing else than the tender, extravagant, solitary, paranoic-critical Camembert of time and space".

In his later years, Dali spent more time at business

meetings than in his studio. "Dali sleeps best," he would say, "after receiving a tremendous quantity of cheques." Judging from his numerous commercials he must have been an habitual late riser. He endorsed everything from perfume to brandy; furniture to body-freezing schemes.

His painting was usually confined to one, lucrative commission a year and he spent as much time as possible relaxing at his home near Cadaques – complete with penis-shaped swimming pool. Dali enjoyed swimming in the testicle area.

"This is where all creation of the world is swirled around and spat out as ideas," he would tell his house guests.

In later life, the man who had teased the art world with his brilliance retreated into a shambling physical shell. He suffered from Parkinson's Disease, depression and poor nutrition, and when in 1984 his 12th century castle at Pubol, near Barcelona, caught fire he was badly burned. He ended his days back at his birthplace in Figueras. There, unable to leave his wheelchair, he was reduced to being fed through a tube until his death in January 1989 at the age of 84.

It is not the way Dali should be remembered. He brought a much-needed vitality to the crusty world of collectable art, and his carefree attitude to forgeries was at once a scandal and a breath of fresh air.

UNITY MITFORD

Did Adolf Hitler father a secret love child? That is the astonishing question posed by historians who have investigated the scandalous life of one of Hitler's most ardent admirers, the aristocratic Englishwoman, Unity Mitford.

Unity was born in August 1914, the month that World War I began, and was christened with the second name Valkyrie, in an eerie prophecy of her Germanic infatuation. Her father, Lord Redesdale, had three other daughters: Diana, who went on to marry fascist Sir Oswald Mosley, and noted authoresses Nancy and Jessica. Sir Oswald and his wife were ordered by Winston Churchill to be incarcerated for the duration of World War II because of their Nazi sympathies. By then Unity was also in a 'prison' of her own making ...

Like her sisters, Unity was brought up in an aristocratic mid-war time warp. As Britain suffered the ravages of the Depression, she lived the life of a country gentlewoman, wanting for nothing at her father's mansion in Oxfordshire. The prettiest of debutantes, she would attend dances with a pet grass snake, Enid, slung around her neck. She also liked to shock her hosts by drawing her pet rat, Ratula, out of her pocket at lavish balls. Her most shocking activities, however, occurred when she visited Germany for the first time at the age of eighteen and witnessed the first Nuremburg rally after the Nazis seized power.

Unity Mitford and sister Diana surrounded by adoring Nazi officers.

Having seen the new German leader hold sway over his supporters, Unity said breathlessly: "The first moment I saw Adolf Hitler I knew there was no one else I would rather meet."

Unity returned to England at the age of nineteen and persuaded her father to allow her to continue her education in Germany. She enrolled in a Munich finishing school, the aim of which was 'to nourish the body and soul of young females in preparation for the life which awaits them outside these portals'. Her aim was more direct, however. It was to meet her hero, Hitler.

The young Miss Mitford haunted Hitler's favourite hangouts until, on 9 February 1935, she was dining alone at the Osteria Bavaria restaurant when she was spotted by the Führer, who sent over an aide to invite her to join his table. She needed no second invitation, and in the ensuing weeks she steadily worked her way into the German dictator's inner circle.

At first suspected of being a British spy, the petite blonde entranced Hitler and won his trust and seemingly his affection. A Nazi diarist at the time, Lienritte von Schirach, wrote:

"Hitler was caught up not only in her beauty but also her social position. I heard her in turn telling him that she admired him and that it was her life's aim that England and Germany should be brought closer together. Hitler fell under her spell and refused to believe those who said she could be a spy. He preferred to trust his own instinctive understanding of people. He also used her to relay his ideas to Britain."

Hitler's infatuation for Unity was returned in even greater measure by the star-struck Unity, as is proved by an interview she gave to a *Sunday Express* correspondent in May 1935:

"Her eyes lit with enthusiasm as she spoke of Hitler. 'The hours I have spent in his company,' she said, 'are some of the most impressive in my life. The entire German nation is lucky to have such a great personality at its head.' As I left her in the students' home in which she has lived for the last year, she raised her arm in the Nazi salute and cried: 'Heil Hitler!'"

Further evidence of the closeness between the former English debutante and the former German corporal was provided by Hitler's armaments minister, Albert Speer:

"She was highly in love with him. It was hero worship of the highest order. I doubt whether he ever did more than take her hand in his but she was the only woman whose opinions he listened to. In discussions over tea, she would always be willing to argue a point, to try to make him see something another way. He would be tolerant and always willing to listen."

The words of Speer, appointed by Hitler as architect of his 'Thousand Year Reich', prove how firmly entrenched Unity had now become in Hitler's inner circle. He sent his staff car to collect her for teatime meetings each afternoon. She visited the so-called 'Eagle's Nest', his mountain retreat high above Berchtesgaden. A naive propagandist for the Nazi cause, she even addressed Nazi rallies. In one speech, she told a cheering crowd that she thought Dachau concentration camp was an ideal home for the Jews and that the other 'lesser races' of the east could only be subdued under the Führer.

On a visit home to England in 1936 she had to be rescued by police at a pro-Nazi rally in Hyde Park, where protesters tried to throw her in the Serpentine river. She was also nearly lynched at a 'Save Spain' rally, where she marched with pro-Franco mobs against supporters of a democratic Spain that was slowly dying under the heel of tyranny.

Upon her return to Munich, Hitler ordered his personal secretary Martin Bormann to help her choose a new apartment in the fashionable Agnesstrasse and to have it redecorated in the most lavish style. Whether this was intended as Hitler's secret love nest will never be known. Hitler already had a mistress, Eva Braun, whom Unity never met but who was known to be bitterly jealous of her English rival. Indeed, Unity's relationship with Hitler was so intimate that in 1938 Lord Redesdale was forced to issue a statement: "There is not, nor has there ever been, any question of an engagement between my daughter and Herr Hitler."

Yet rumours of an affair between them persisted. Most astonishingly, in 1994 a woman in her fifties, by now living in Austria, claimed to be Unity's secret love child, allegedly born just before World War II.

Unity Mitford's dreams of a pact between the Aryan brotherhood of Britain and Germany were shattered on 1 September 1939 when German forces marched into Poland. Two days later Britain declared war on Germany and a distraught Unity was forced to choose between the land of her birth and the country of her adoption. She chose Britain.

Unity first visited the *gauleiter* of Munich, Adolf Wagner, and handed him a brown envelope. "She wept," recalled Wagner. "She could not speak. In the envelope was her Nazi Party badge, a picture of Hitler and a letter to the Führer in which she said she could no longer find a reason to live."

She then went to a park in the centre of Munich known as the English Garden. There she drew out a small calibre handgun and put it to her temple. She pulled the trigger.

Unity slumped on a bench in front of the Haus der Kunst, one of the first neoclassical architectural triumphs of the Thousand Year Reich. Park officials rushed to her side and were astonished to find that she was not dead. In hospital, surgeons discovered that the bullet had lodged in her brain, not far enough to kill her, too far to risk its removal.

Hitler was at her side within 24 hours. The dictator was visibly shaken. There were tears in his eyes on 8 November 1939 – the last time he ever saw her – when he agreed to her request to be returned to Britain as soon as she was able to make the journey.

The Führer had a railway carriage converted into a mobile hospital so that Unity, accompanied by doctors and nurses, could be ferried through Switzerland and Southern France and thence by boat to England. She arrived at Folkestone in the spring of 1940, just before Hitler unleashed his *blitzkrieg* on France, Holland and Belgium.

Unity Mitford had returned to a country which, having once regarded her as eccentric, now despised her. Despite calls for her internment, she was allowed to live out the war recuperating at her family's Scottish island, Inchkenneth. She never recovered. Permanently confused, she survived for nine years in a kind of twilight zone. One of the most glittering figures of her age, Unity died disgraced and unmourned in 1948.

PRINCESS MARGARET

Princess Margaret was more precocious, more daring, more fun-loving than her sister Elizabeth, heiress to the British throne. She was also more of a flirt. When Margaret was introduced to the dashing RAF war hero Peter Townsend, she used all her feminine wiles to attract and keep his attention ... even though he was 29 and she was just 14 years of age.

Everyone believed that the way Princess Margaret looked at Group Captain Townsend was simply a schoolgirl crush – but that immediate, dangerous spark of attraction was to change her life irrevocably and end in heartache for her.

In 1947 Margaret's father, King George VI, took Townsend on as an equerry within the royal household. Margaret, by then aged seventeen, was overjoyed that she could see more of her secret beau. The closeness which was to develop between the impressionable princess and the handsome flier more than twice her age was reinforced by the fact that Townsend was to act virtually as 'minder' to her while her sister Elizabeth concentrated on her more onerous duties with her new consort Prince Philip.

Margaret continued to harbour a deep yearning for Townsend as a series of overseas visits threw them even closer together. The RAF officer would travel alone, leaving his wife Rosemary at their home in the grounds of Windsor Castle. In that prudish, post-war

Forbidden love: Princess Margaret and Peter Townsend.

age, Margaret thought she had no chance of finding happiness with her married hero. Then in 1951 came her chance: Townsend's marriage hit the rocks.

He told Margaret of his divorce plans on 14 August 1951, just four days before her twenty-first birthday, when the pair were out riding in the romantic setting of the wooded grounds of Balmoral Castle. Margaret's heart leapt with joy. The stage was set for romance – and scandal – to blossom.

In February 1952 King George VI died. Margaret, who doted on her father and was in turn his favourite, was heartbroken. While her sister Elizabeth acceded to the throne, Margaret moved to Clarence House, taking on the effective role of companion to her widowed mother. This made it even easier for the illicit lovebirds to meet because in May the Queen Mother appointed Peter Townsend as comptroller of her household.

"We found increasing solace in each other's company," Townsend later wrote coyly.

Inevitably the couple had to break the news of their love affair to the Queen – and ask the question: Could they wed? The moment of truth came when Margaret and Townsend, by now further promoted to Queen's Equerry, were invited to dinner at Buckingham Palace. The Queen Mother was supportive, and the Queen was sympathetic, although her husband seemed less committed.

Margaret was sufficiently encouraged by the reaction that she even asked Peter Townsend to help decorate her quarters at Clarence House, believing that he would one day share them with her.

The lovebirds would slip away to dine quietly together. Sometimes they would stay at a friend's house, sometimes they would simply go to the cinema together. They were never recognised by the general public or the press. However, they themselves never recognised the serious obstacles they would have to overcome to be able to fly in the face of centuries of tradition.

Townsend only realised the scale of the problem when he told his friend, the Queen's senior advisor Sir Alan Lascelles, that he planned to wed. Lascelles turned on the young officer and barked: "You must be either bad or mad!"

Suddenly the lovers' rose-tinted world was turning black. The Queen's senior adviser ordered Townsend to have nothing more to do with the vulnerable young princess, and instead to accept a posting abroad. Lascelles then went to the Queen and reminded her that in order to wed, Margaret needed the consent of Parliament and of all Britain's dominions, and this she probably would not get. He also pointed to the intractability of the Church of England over remarriage of divorced persons, and that the head of the Church of England is, of course, the Queen herself.

One by one, the Queen, Prince Philip, their advisers and government leaders all opposed the unhappy lovers. All were haunted by recollections of the abdication of Edward VIII in 1936 after he fell in love with divorcée Wallis Simpson.

While all this was going on, the British public remained blissfully unaware of the looming scandal. They were concentrating on the most glittering royal occasion in living memory: the Coronation of the new Queen.

When Coronation Day dawned on 2 June 1953, almost all eyes at Westminster Abbey were on the young Elizabeth II. Princess Margaret, however, had eyes only for Peter Townsend who stood a couple of paces away from her. Margaret, bejewelled and radiant, turned slightly, looked up at him and gently stretched out her white-gloved hand to pick a piece of fluff from his RAF uniform. As her hand brushed proudly across his tunic, an eagle-eyed American reporter spotted this simple act of love. The rumours he had heard since arriving in London were now confirmed. Princess Margaret had given the game away.

The following day the *Journal American* carried the tale. It was quickly picked up by other newspapers around the world. Only the British press remained silent. And when the first London newspaper ran the story, it was to deny it! *The Sunday People* reported: "It is quite unthinkable that a royal princess, third in line of succession, should even contemplate marriage with a man who has been through the divorce courts."

Buckingham Palace got around the Townsend-Margaret 'problem' with unwarranted brutality. Princess Margaret was dispatched with the Queen Mother on a tour of Rhodesia, while Lascelles finally got his way and 'exiled' Townsend to the trumped-up posting of air attaché in Brussels.

Every editor in Fleet Street had marked in his diary the date 21 August 1955 – the day of Princess Margaret's 25th birthday, the age when a member of the Royal Family may marry without the monarch's consent. They correctly guessed that this was what Margaret was planning, although she still hoped to get her sister's blessing.

The month was marked by a series of royal summits. The Queen, Prince Philip and the Queen Mother told Margaret that if her marriage went ahead she would have to renounce her rights to the throne and her income from the Civil List. She would also have to live abroad for a period, as an effective outcast.

Townsend was recalled from Brussels on 12 October and met Margaret, who had rushed by train from Balmoral. They are believed to have been reunited in the privacy of Clarence House for just two hours. Then they parted again to await the verdict of the Queen, her advisers and her ministers. Their various pronouncements were perhaps best summed up by a thundering leader column in *The Times* which, fulminating with hypocritical outrage, condemned the marriage plans as damaging to the Queen's position as the symbol of goodness in family life.

The couple themselves reacted in a straightforward manner. They met up at a friend's house in London's Knightsbridge and got hopelessly drunk. The following morning they woke up with sore heads and drafted one of the most moving official statements ever released by the palace. An approved version was put out on a cold, miserable Monday, 31 October. It read:

"I would like it to be known that I have decided not to marry Group Captain Peter Townsend. I have been aware that subject to my renouncing my rights of succession it might have been possible for me to contract a civil marriage. But mindful of the Church's teaching that a Christian marriage is indissoluble and conscious of my duty to the Commonwealth, I have resolved to put these considerations before any others. I have reached the decision entirely alone, and in doing so I have been strengthened by the unfailing support and devotion of Group Captain Peter Townsend. I am grateful for the concern of all those who have constantly prayed for my happiness."

Peter Townsend quietly faded from the scene. He went into self-imposed exile in France and married a Belgian girl, Marie-Luce, who bore him three children.

Princess Margaret threw herself into a round of partying and high-living which ended when she married photographer Anthony Armstrong Jones at Westminster Abbey on 6 May 1960. They had two children but the marriage ended in bitter acrimony. After flings with social high-fliers Robin Douglas-Home and Roddy Llewellyn, Margaret determined to end the marriage.

Now the Queen had to come to terms with the

previously unthinkable: divorce within the Royal Family.

Edward VIII's marriage to divorcée Wallis Simpson had been one thing; Margaret's bid to marry divorcée Peter Townsend was another – but this was to be a divorce by the sister of the Queen, head of the Church of England. It was to be the first divorce by an immediate member of the Royal Family since the head-chopping days of Henry VIII. It was a constitutional dilemma that reminded Queen Elizabeth of the agonising she and her family had undergone when the Peter Townsend scandal had broken.

The eventual divorce of Princess Margaret in 1978 did not, however, shock the nation, as had been feared. It only proved to the public, as sadly it did for Margaret herself, that the sacrifice she had made to avert a scandal over her affair with Peter Townsend all those years before had been entirely in vain. She had forsaken the great love of her life ... for nothing.

LANA TURNER

Jerry Geisler's home telephone number was known to most Hollywood stars. As California's most prestigious lawyer, he was the man they called at the slightest whiff of trouble, from traffic violations to small-print problems in a contract. Geisler always liked them to know that they had access to him at all times.

On this particular night, 4 April 1958, the lawyer was celebrating Good Friday quietly at his apartment. When the phone rang at 10 pm he assumed that it was a work call. He could hardly have guessed how the next few hours would unfold.

The woman on the other end of the line was Lana Turner, one of the biggest names on the silver screen. Yet the assured, silky voice that wowed movie fans across the world now sounded desperate, almost frantic.

"Something terrible has happened," she told Geisler. "John Stompanato is dead. He is here."

Geisler wasted no time getting to her home in North Bedford Drive, Beverley Hills. He made it shortly after the arrival of the local police chief, Clinton Anderson, and immediately began reassuring Lana and her fifteen-year-old daughter, Cheryl Crane.

It didn't take long to work out what had happened.

"Please let me say I did it," the actress begged. "Lana, don't," replied the officer. "We already know it was Cheryl."

Lana Turner ... her violent lover was stabbed to death.

The 33-year-old Stompanato – Lana's lover for the past year – had been stabbed to death with a wicked-looking, eight inch carving knife. Cheryl told how she arrived home from boarding school for the Easter holidays to find the couple in the middle of a blazing row. She begged her mother to kick Stompanato out, but Lana refused, saying she was "deathly afraid" of him. Cheryl promised her she would stay close to her side that night.

Lana certainly had good reason to fear Stompanato. He was the 'muscle' for gangster Mickey Cohen, himself an associate of the big-league mobster Bugsy Siegel. With friends like these, Stompanato boasted that he feared no one. He made a modest income from theft and fencing stolen goods, using a furniture store and pet shop to give him a credible business front. However, the cash that came in was never enough for his extravagant needs.

One way he got around this was to attach himself to wealthy, attractive women prepared to bankroll him. In Hollywood slang this made him a 'fee-male' (it was the women who always paid the fees) but it didn't deter Lana from entering into a passionate affair. Like his three previous wives, she was at first captivated by his classical good looks and winning charm.

Stompanato began wooing her in April 1957, by sending a succession of bouquets to the studio where she was filming *The Lady Takes Flyer*. The flowers carried no message – only the name John Steele and a phone number. When Lana rang and spoke to her mysterious admirer, he told her that they had a mutual friend in Ava Gardner. It was a lie but she didn't bother to call Ava, who was away at the time.

At first Lana politely turned down his offers of lunch, saying that she was too busy. But her curiosity was already nagging away and when John Steele began mailing packages containing her favourite records, she was hooked. How could he know such personal detail? In a moment of recklessness she decided to give him her home phone number.

Later she admitted:"That is how the blackest period in my life began. What happened I can never forget, but why it happened I'll never really understand."

Perhaps the truth is that Lana was lonely and just wanted to have a man about the place. When she met John Stompanato she was 38 and already had four broken marriages behind her. The previous husbands – bandleader Artie Shaw, Cheryl's father Steve Crane, millionaire Bob Topping and fellow film star Lex Barker – had failed to meet her expectations and none lasted more than a few years. Another drawback was that her hectic filming schedule restricted opportunities to forge a solid relationship.

By the mid 40s Lana was among America's top ten women earners. Hollywood folklore has it that she was discovered at the age of fifteen while sitting in a Sunset Boulevard café. She quickly made her debut in the appropriately named *A Star is Born*. Other big parts would follow in *Peyton Place*, *Johnny Eager*, *The Bad and the Beautiful*, *Madame X* and *The*

Postman Always Rings Twice.

It was this success that soured her relationship with Stompanato. He became jealous of her fame and tried to assert his dominance over her with savage beatings. When the rage expired he would once again become the gentle, caring lover she had once known.

"I had only myself to blame for getting involved, too deeply involved," Lana admitted later. "By the time I had gotten in over my head, I didn't have a clue about how I was going to get rid of the man. I just hoped he would go peacefully. But underlying everything was my shame. I was so ashamed that I didn't want anyone to know my predicament, how foolish I had been, how I had taken him at face value and been completely duped."

"If I ever tried to picture how it would end, I would have a vision of myself, dead or mutilated, and I cold see no other way out. I knew what the man was capable of."

Towards the end of 1957 Lana made one carefully planned attempt to shake off Stompanato. She arrived in Britain to make *Another Time, Another Place* with a rising young star called Sean Connery.

The plot demanded lots of love scenes, and observers on the set soon realised that Connery and Turner had become close on personal, as well as professional terms. The last thing Lana wanted was a jealous John Stompanato storming around off camera and she banned him from joining her on the set in England.

It made no difference. Stomapanato borrowed his

air fare from Mickey Cohen and turned up to haunt her.

When she barred him from the set, he waited at her rented house in the plush North London suburb of Hampstead and confronted her. A row blew up – partly because Lana was so scathing of his ambition to become a film producer – and Stompanato attacked her, almost smothering her with a pillow.

The next day he was waiting at the house again with a chilling warning.

"I'm not kidding around," he said. "I can take care of your mother and Cheryl too. Don't think I won't do it. I can have it done. No one will ever know where it came from."

The third day Stompanato sneaked onto the set and pulled a gun on Sean Connery. With reactions that James Bond himself would surely have admired, Connery floored him with a sweetly-delivered right.

A couple of days later, after Lana telephoned Scotland Yard pleading for help, Stompanato was quietly escorted onto a plane home.

With her lover 3,000 miles away, Lana longed to be with him again. She wrote one letter which included the lines: "To say how much you are and have been missed is almost impossible. I dare not, even to myself, admit how much." They had a reunion water-skiing in Acapulco, and she presented him with a keepsake – a bracelet bearing the inscription in Spanish: "My sweet love. Remember a piece of my heart will be with you always – Lana."

Yet little in the relationship had changed.

Stompanato still flew into violent tantrums during which he would point his pistol at her and warn that one day she would be killed.

The Good Friday argument came to a head after Lana discovered he had been lying to her about his age (he claimed to be five years older than her when he was acutally five years younger). In an outpouring of anger and frustration she accused him of bleeding her financially and cried: "I can't go on like this. I want you to leave me alone."

Stompanato smirked back: "If I tell you to jump, you jump. If I tell you to hop, you hop. No matter what you do I'll never let you go."

Then, as she stood in the doorway of her bedroom, Cheryl Crane heard the threat that made her decide to kill Lana's tormentor.

"I'll get you if it takes a day, a week, a month or a year," Stompanato was saying. "If I can't do it myself, I'll find someone who will. That's my business."

Quickly Cheryl rushed to the kitchen, grabbed the knife and stormed back to the warring couple. In one movement she plunged it into Stompanato's heart.

Under astute questioning from Jerry Geisler, Lana later told the inquest:

"Mr. Stompanato stumbled forward, turned around and fell on his back. He choked, his hands on his throat. I ran to him and lifted up his sweater. It was the blood ... he made a horrible noise in his throat." She paused to dry her tears and take a sip of water. Then she continued: "I tried to breathe air into his semi-open lips, my mouth against his ... he was dying."

The verdict of justifiable homicide was delivered inside 30 minutes. It was never in any doubt. Cheryl Crane was released from a juvenile prison and she and her mother tried to resume a normal life. For Lana, however, though the search for the man of her dreams was a fruitless one. After seven failed marriages she decided it was better, after all, to live alone.

SIR ANTHONY BLUNT

The cold war of the 50s and 60s was the golden age of spying. Armies of intelligence agents across the superpower divide did battle daily to penetrate the enemy and unmask traitors on their own side. It was the stuff of pop thrillers and schoolboy comic strips. Consequently it made the fictional British agent James Bond a household name around the world.

However, the Bond adventures – readable as they were – were a million miles from the reality of intelligence gathering. The aim of the Great Game, as it was called, was simple. Pilfer a few top secret government documents, copy them and drop them in a dead letter box for your controller. Then return the originals and survive to spy another day.

It is called high treason and in the United Kingdom it remains the only offence still to carry the death penalty. Even today the two arms of the British Secret Service – MI5 (the Security Service) and MI6 (the Secret Intelligence Service) – remain obsessive about the possibility of a traitor in their ranks.

And no wonder. Britain's post-war history of spy scandals makes grim reading. The memory of Kim Philby, Guy Burgess and Donald Maclean, all of whom betrayed their country for years before fleeing to start new lives in the Soviet Union, still rankles in the corridors of Whitehall. Perhaps even more painful for UK spymasters is the memory of the 'Fourth

Spy in Buckingham Palace: Anthony Blunt with the Queen.

Man': art historian Anthony Blunt, described by intelligence expert and author Chapman Pincher as 'one of the most damaging spies ever to operate in Britain'.

The Blunt fiasco is a story of cover-ups and hypocrisy, a story in which he was handed honours galore, courted by the Establishment and even admitted to the exclusive Royal Court as Surveyor of the Queen's Pictures. That he achieved much of this after MI5 had secretly unmasked him as a double agent remains one of the most shameful episodes in the history of British intelligence.

Born in 1907, the son of a London clergyman, Blunt won a scholarship to Trinity College, Cambridge, in 1926. He became convinced of the Marxist cause during deep conversations with his friend Guy Burgess, a fellow homosexual, and when Burgess took up a career as a British agent Blunt became recruiter-in-chief for the Red cause at Cambridge. Later, in 1940, he himself graduated to MI5 (after earlier being black-listed as a security risk) from the Army Intelligence Corps. From then on any classified information that came his way was routed straight to Moscow.

Blunt left MI5 at the end of the war, but remained ideologically close to Burgess, Philby and Maclean. When Burgess told him that British counter-intelligence suspected Maclean of being a double-agent, Blunt resolved to help in any way he could. It was he who helped set up Burgess and Maclean's defection in the summer of 1951, controlled by his old

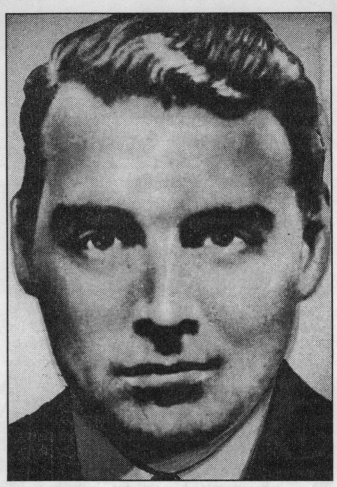

Spy on the run ... handsome Guy Burgess.

contacts at the Soviet embassy in London.

Later Blunt denied that he supplied the tip-off to the two traitors, which even gave them the date they were due to be pulled in by MI5. As we shall see, that tip may have come from an even higher authority.

After the sensational defections, Blunt naturally came under suspicion because of his close ties with Burgess. He managed to bluster his way through a series of interrogations until he finally confessed in 1964. His statements were offered in return for a promise of immunity from prosecution. He also agreed to help where he could in the task of rooting out other moles inside British intelligence.

Incredibly, the decision to give Blunt this immunity was taken by the then Attorney-General, Sir John Hobson, without the knowledge of the Prime Minister of the day, Sir Alec Douglas Home.

MI5 argued that Blunt should be allowed to continue in life as if nothing had happened. His co-operation was all-important to their counter-intelligence strategy. The Queen was informed that her art expert was a spy but accepted the advice to leave him in place.

So Blunt continued to enjoy his juicy Establishment niches. He was a Knight Commander of the Royal Victorian Order, Slade Professor of Fine Art at both Oxford and Cambridge Universities and recipient of honorary degrees at Bristol, Durham and Paris. He enjoyed the respect of his peers and was in much demand on all the right social circuits.

It wasn't until 1979 that Blunt was at last exposed

Traitor Kim Philby cost many agents their lives.

by Prime Minister Margaret Thatcher in the House of Commons, confirming allegations made against him by the author Andrew Boyle. Blunt was immediately stripped of his knighthood and sacked as palace art adviser.

Yet in some quarters he was still treated as a venerable academic to be respected and admired. His farce of a press conference was confined to journalists from *The Guardian* and *The Times* and after a few minutes he trotted off into the boardroom at *The Times* to be entertained over a lunch of trout and white wine.

The *Daily Express*, which had first broken the 'Cambridge Ring' spy scandal exposing Philby, Burgess and Maclean, observed tartly: "Professor Blunt would not have been offered so much as a stale kipper in the Express offices." It was a view shared by most ordinary Britons. They found it incomprehensible that a man who had so coldly betrayed his country for communism should still be living the good life of capitalism.

Blunt died in 1983 leaving many questions about his true role unanswered. The most intriguing of these relates to the so-called 'Fifth Man', the highest ranking double agent ever to have penetrated British Intelligence. The truth about his identity may never be known, but the finger points firmly to Sir Roger Hollis, the Director General of MI5 between 1956 and 1965.

The allegation against Hollis was first made by Chapman Pincher in his book *Their Trade Is*

Treachery. He claimed that Mrs Thatcher was warned in 1980 of another potentially explosive scandal within MI5 and that Hollis's name was given to her. She authorised a secret inquiry by former Cabinet Secretary Sir Burke Trend, whose mandate was to decide whether Hollis had been a double agent for more than 30 years. Sir Burke cleared him and Mrs Thatcher passed the result of the investigation to parliament.

If MI5 hoped that was the end of the embarrassment, it was wrong. Pincher stuck by his story and within months further backing came from Peter Wright, an MI5 'mole-catcher' who had headed a top-secret internal probe into communist infiltration of the security service. He said: "Those of us intimately concerned with the investigation believed that Hollis ... had been a long-term Soviet penetration agent in MI5." Wright acknowledged he couldn't prove the allegation but added: "Intelligence-wise, it is 99 per cent certain he was a spy."

No one will ever know the cost in lives of Western field agents resulting directly from the treachery of Blunt, Burgess, Philby, Maclean and perhaps Hollis. In these days of peace between the superpowers, many people now regard the acts as only of historical interest.

THE PROFUMO AFFAIR

Cliveden is a magnificent mansion atop a hill overlooking the River Thames, near Maidenhead, Berkshire. It is now a luxurious country hotel but in the 1960s it was the home of Lord Astor, one of the richest men in England.

At weekends Lord Astor would invite the royal, the noble, the rich and the famous to join him for lavish parties. The guests were the most influential and respectable people in the land.

Less respectable, perhaps, were the guests at other weekend parties which were held elsewhere on the Cliveden estate. They took place at a cottage in the grounds – a cottage that Stephen Ward leased from Lord Astor at a token rent of £1 a year. Ward was a society osteopath with a host of impressive names on his client list. He was also a procurer of young ladies for many of those clients and for his circle of free-loving friends ...

On one balmy July evening in 1961, the two parties of 'weekenders' – Lord Astor's and Ward's – met in the grounds of Cliveden, and the most infamous political sex scandal ever to shake British politics was launched on its inauspicious course ...

That Saturday evening, Ward and his guests were using the swimming pool to cool down after a day of partying and drinking. Christine Keeler, a nineteen-year-old showgirl and model, was wearing a borrowed swimsuit far too large for her, so Ward

John Profumo: A glittering career destroyed by lust.

suggested she remove it altogether. Laughing, Keeler stripped naked and dived into the pool.

Upon getting out on the other side, the shapely showgirl found herself face to face with two guests from the main house who had wandered down to the pool to investigate the girlish giggles. One was Lord Astor and the other John Profumo, the War Minister in the ruling Conservative Government. Embarrassed, Keeler grabbed a towel in a vain attempt to cover her beautiful torso and her blushes. Profumo's wife, actress Valerie Hobson, arrived on the scene and, ironically, offered her own swimsuit to Keeler. Introductions were then made and Ward's party was invited to join Astor and the Profumos at the main house. There Profumo led the shy model on a guided tour of the stately home.

Christine Keeler returned to London that night but the following day, a sweltering Sunday, she returned to Cliveden accompanied by two other girls and Stephen Ward's friend Eugene Ivanov, the assistant naval attaché at the Soviet Embassy. From morning onwards, the two parties of 'weekenders' again gathered around the swimming pool, where Profumo and Ivanov seemed to be vying for the attention of the sexy showgirl.

Without much difficulty, Profumo persuaded Christine Keeler to give him her telephone number. It was Ivanov, however, who accompanied her back to London on the Sunday night. They went to Ward's flat in Wimpole Mews and fell into bed together.

Over the months, Ward and Ivanov became the

Stephen Ward: Society osteopath died in police cells.

best of friends. The Russian found Ward a highly useful contact and reported back on his meeting with Profumo. The osteopath, on his part, seemed to have a genuine affection for Ivanov – although he did try to keep himself in the clear by informing an MI5 contact about their meetings. The British agent was particularly alarmed at the news that Keeler was a friend of both a Russian spy and the War Minister.

John Profumo seemed unashamed that he was dating a showgirl. He drove her around London in his ministerial limousine and, although she did not find the balding politician particularly attractive, she was awed by his power and prestige. When his wife Valerie Hobson was away, he would have sex with her at his own grand home overlooking Regents Park. On other occasions, he would meet her at Ward's flat. Unbeknown to him, so would Ivanov.

Profumo's indiscretion soon sparked rumours. It was difficult to ignore what was going on when, no sooner had a government limousine pulled away from Ward's mews house, than a Soviet Embassy staff car drew up! Profumo was quietly warned off by MI5 – and foolishly wrote her what he planned to be a 'goodbye' letter. It read in part:

"Darling, In great haste and because I can get no reply from your phone. Alas something's blown up tomorrow night and I can't therefore make it. I'm terribly sorry, especially as I leave the next day for various trips and then a holiday, so won't be able to see you again until some time in September. Blast it. Please take great care of yourself and don't run away. Love, J."

Soviet spy Eugene Ivanov shared a mistress with Profumo.

Throughout this period, Christine Keeler was being harassed by a former boyfriend, West Indian 'singer' and drug dealer Lucky Gordon. For a while, she escaped to America with her friend and fellow model, Mandy Rice-Davies. But upon their return, Gordon came calling again, and hit her on more than one occasion. Keeler illegally bought a pistol for her protection.

Another West Indian, Johnny Edgecombe, became Christine Keeler's lover in 1962. Insanely jealous, Lucky Gordon attacked him in a club and Edgecombe retaliated by slashing Gordon's face from his chin to his forehead. Christine went into hiding at Ward's mews house – but on 14 December Edgecombe tracked her down there. He was carrying her own pistol.

Keeler and Mandy Rice-Davies, who was also staying at the house, refused the raging Edgecombe entry. He tried to shoot the door lock off, then fired a shot at Keeler through a window. Neighbours called the police, who were swiftly followed by a number of journalists. Edgecombe had fled the scene but was later arrested at his West London flat.

Suddenly the rumours and the gossip that had circulated about Keeler and Profumo the previous year began to be repeated. This time there was a legitimate story for the press to report: the shooting in Wimpole Mews and the court case that followed it.

On 14 March 1963 Edgecombe was found not guilty of assaulting Lucky Gordon but was sentenced to seven years in jail for possessing a firearm. Keeler had disappeared to Spain just before the case. Since she was one of the prosecution's main witnesses, this was unfortunate for the police. It was more unfortunate for John Profumo. For whereas this minor fracas in a London backstreet might have passed unreported, it raised the interest of the press to fever pitch.

Keeler had by now told her story to several journalists and even to politicians. It became clear to Profumo that he could keep silent no longer. Astonishingly, in an act of bravado that was to wreak his final downfall and damnation, Profumo decided to brazen out the entire scandal. He saw Conservative Party leaders and made a statement to the Attorney General – denying most emphatically that he had ever had an affair with Keeler. He threatened newspapers that if the allegations were repeated he would sue for libel. Moreover, when prominent Labour politician George Wigg stood up in the House of Commons on 21 March 1963 and, using parliamentary privilege, raised a question about the cabinet minister and the model, Profumo replied with a statement to the House the following day. In part it read:

"My wife and I first met Miss Keeler at a house party in July 1961 at Cliveden. Among a number of people there was Dr Stephen Ward, whom we already knew slightly, and a Mr Ivanov, who was an attaché at the Russian Embassy ... Between July and December 1961, I met Miss Keeler on about half a dozen occasions at Dr Ward's flat when I called to see him and his friends. Miss Keeler and I were on friendly terms. There was no impropriety whatsoever in my acquaintance with Miss Keeler ... I shall not hesitate to issue writs for libel and slander if scandalous allegations are made or repeated outside the House."

The die was cast. The Minister of the Crown had lied to the House of Commons and to the nation. MI5 were astonished but muffled; the Labour opposition were enraged; the press could not forgive him. All were out for his blood.

So too, strangely, was his old friend Stephen Ward who, fearing that he was being set up as a liar, pimp or even an enemy agent, sought a meeting with George Wigg and told him everything. He sought a meeting with Prime Minister Harold Macmillan and was allowed an audience with his secretary Timothy Bligh, with an MI5 officer sitting in. Ward claimed that he had long ago informed MI5 of the affairs between Ivanov, Keeler and Profumo. MI5 simply denied it – and Ward realised with increasing panic that he was to be the 'fall guy' for the entire sordid scandal.

Ward was talking, Keeler was talking, and the press were talking to anyone connected with either of them. Profumo was on holiday in Venice with his wife when the summons came from the Prime Minister's office: Return to London immediately to be interviewed by the Lord Chancellor, Lord Dilhorne. The disgraced minister could prevaricate no longer. He confessed to his wife, returned to London and, on 5 June, resigned. His letter to Macmillan still

Showgirl Christine Keeler with procurer
Stephen Ward.

attempted vainly to excuse his dishonour, referring to Keeler only as the missing 'witness' in the Edgecombe court case. Profumo's letter read in part:

"Dear Prime Minister ... I allowed myself to think that my personal association with that witness was by comparison of minor importance only. In my statement, I said there had been no impropriety in this association. To my very deep regret, I have to admit that this was not true and that I misled you, my colleagues and the House ... I have come to realise that, by this deception, I have been guilty of a grave misdemeanour ... I cannot remain a member of your administration, nor of the House of Commons ... I cannot tell you of my deep remorse for the embarrassment I have caused you ..."

John Profumo had lost his career and his honour. Stephen Ward, however, was to lose his life. The scapegoat for the scandal that had almost brought down a government was arrested and charged with living off the immoral earnings of Christine Keeler and Mandy Rice-Davies. On the eve of a guilty verdict against him, Ward took an overdose of Nembutal tablets, leaving a suicide note that read:

"It's not only fear. It's a wish not to let them get me. I'd rather get myself."

The judge in his trial postponed sentence on Ward until he recovered sufficiently to appear again in the dock. He never did. Ward died on 3 August 1963, having paid the ultimate price for a government's shame and another man's folly.

8 June 1961: MI5 quiz osteopath Stephen Ward about his friendship with Soviet Embassy attaché Captain Eugene Ivanov.

8 July: Christine Keeler meets War Minister John Profumo. Keeler begins an affair with Profumo and also sleeps with Ivanov.

9 August: Profumo, warned by MI5, writes Keeler a 'farewell' letter.

14 December 1962: Another of Keeler's lovers, West Indian Johnny Edgecombe, is arrested after a shooting incident at Ward's flat while Keeler is staying there.

22 January 1963: Keeler tells the story of Profumo, Ivanov and herself to a newspaper.

29 January: Ivanov leaves Britain.

14 March: Edgecombe is sentenced to seven years in jail.

22 March: Profumo tells the Commons: "There was no impropriety."

23 March: Police launch an investigation into Ward's involvement with prostitutes.

20 May: Ward canvasses his friends, including MPs, and accuses Profumo of lying to the House.

5 June: Profumo resigns.

8 June: Ward is arrested and charged with living off immoral earnings.

21 June: Prime Minister Harold Macmillan appoints judge Lord Denning to inquire into the security aspects of the scandal.

30 July: While standing trial, Ward takes an overdose of barbiturates in his cell.

3 August: Ward dies in hospital.

MICK JAGGER

Mick Jagger was the *bête noir* of the 60s Establishment. Long haired, sexually provocative on stage and hero-in-chief to a generation of teenage rebels, he was every parent's nightmare. Yet despite his devil-may-care image, Jagger was really one of life's worriers. A thinker and a carer, he yearned for a quiet life offstage and perhaps secretly envied the ordered certainty of the middle classes he publicly repudiated.

The Rolling Stones had, though, crafted themselves a shocking and outrageous image. It was the brainchild of their first manager, Andrew Loog Oldham, who reckoned it was pointless to tag along with the goody-two-shoes publicity enjoyed by the Beatles.

Now Mick was stuck with it. Right-wing politicians believed he was a dangerous anarchist, parents saw him as an over-sexed pervert and the police hierarchy regarded the band as a bunch of no-good hippie layabouts in great need of some discipline.

So when 23-year-old Mick got busted for drugs one wet weekend in February 1967, the Establishment uncorked the champagne and settled down happily to watch this rubber-lipped upstart get his come-uppance. If only they could have known the truth – that Jagger took the blame, as a gentleman, to save his girlfriend's skin.

Sex, drugs and rock 'n' roll: Mick Jagger and Keith Richards.

The weekend party at Keith Richards' thatched country cottage, Redlands, near West Wittering, Sussex, had begun with Mick typically on edge. During the drive down in his dark green Aston Martin, he had repeatedly quizzed his lover Marianne Faithfull about what lay ahead. "I don't like it. You know what Keith is ... there's bound to be stuff lying round all over the place."

Marianne only laughed and told him to calm down. She promised that the guests were people he liked: people like Christopher Gibbs, the Chelsea antique dealer, art patron Robert Fraser, Michael Cooper the band's official photographer, Beatle George Harrison and wife Patti, and Nicky Cramer, a well-heeled flower child from the Kings Road.

Mick was still unconvinced. He pointedly asked if another Stone, the drug–crazed Brian Jones, might turn up with a pocket-full of illegal substances. Again Marianne reassured him.

Though she didn't say it, she knew why he was so uptight about the party. Only a few days earlier Mick had been 'turned over' by a Sunday newspaper investigative team and accused of smoking hash and popping amphetamines. Some outrageous quotes had been attributed to him and he was said to have bragged openly about his misdeeds to two undercover reporters at the super-trendy rock club Blazes.

It was a fantastic story ... apart from one important fact. The journalists were a couple of out-of-touch squares for whom one pop star was much like another. The man they'd interviewed was not

Mick Jagger but Brian Jones out on a booze and drugs binge. Jagger had immediately filed a writ for libel, even though his lawyers had warned him of the risk that entailed. Although the newspaper would be hard pushed to mount a defence of its article, it would redouble its efforts to find some genuine dirt.

With this in mind, Mick now felt he would rather be almost anywhere except Keith Richards' place.

Neither could he forget Marianne's own relaxed attitude to popping pills. The couple had been through a furious row during their recent holiday in France when Mick realised she was experimenting with amphetamine tablets, then legal in Europe but outlawed in Britain. If he had realised, as she sat beside him in the Aston, that she still had five of the tablets in her handbag, he would have gone berserk.

As they stopped for petrol that Saturday afternoon, Marianne decided she ought to do something about the 'uppers'. She couldn't bring herself to throw them away so, while Mick was paying the attendant, she swallowed one and looked around for a handy hiding place. On the back seat lay Jagger's hand-made green velvet jacket. She knew he was already bored with it and unlikely to give it an outing at the party. It was as good a place as any.

She and Mick pulled into the driveway of Redlands to find Keith waiting to greet them. The very first topic of conversation got the singer's nerves jangling again. "I just had Brian on the phone," said Keith.

"What did he want?" Jagger's question carried a

hint of despair.

"Dunno. I think he was tripping man. Said he tried to go into the studio to do a backing track but there were black beetles swarming everywhere."

This latest news about the Stones' problem member would dominate Jagger's thoughts for much of the evening, according to distinguished rock writer Philip Norman, who later catalogued the events of that day in fine detail. After dinner he sat down with George Harrison for a heart-to-heart on what to do about Brian.

The drugs had, Mick believed, destroyed Jones' precocious talent. He was now such a loose cannon that his guitar had to be secretly unplugged to prevent him messing up recording sessions. Mick feared it was only a matter of time before Jones was busted by police and the band's plan to conquer the USA would be thwarted by that criminal record.

Jagger's general sense of unease was now overpowering. He had overheard a conversation in which an unfamiliar American dressed in a kaftan and carrying a large briefcase had been waxing lyrical on the latest 'designer' drug.

"You're kidding me," the man was telling Nicky Cramer. "You mean you never heard of demethyl triptomyne?"

Mick asked Keith the guy's name. "Acid King David", he was told. "New guru of mine. Case anyone feels like a little sparkly."

"Not acid, man it's too risky," said Mick. "Especially with these bloody journalists spying on me." Keith told him to cool it. If the police did raid the cottage, there was a choice of three toilets down which the drugs could be flushed away.

After a long lie-in the next day, the party guests brunched on coffee, eggs, Jack Daniels whiskey and Dom Perignon before Keith Richards led them on a meandering walk through woods to a secluded shingle beach. There was a half-hearted attempt to find a house belonging to the surrealist Edward James and then, at about 5.30pm, the company returned to Redlands for a buffet. George Harrison and Patti left early for their Esher bungalow. It turned out to be a smart move.

Later that evening, with Bob Dylan's nasal whine droning out of the stereo, Richard answered the heavy knock at the door. Standing before him, complete with gloves, cane and white-braided cap stood Chief Superintendent Gordon Dineley with a search warrant. He was, he said, looking for illegal substances specified in the Dangerous Drugs Act 1964.

Later Marianne would admit to being overcome by a fit of giggles. Glancing at Jagger's disbelieving face she thought: "Poor Mick. The first time he even has a smell of LSD and half the Sussex police come pouring out of the woodwork."

There were in fact nineteen officers present. They had obviously been tipped off by the resourceful Sunday newspaper, whose journalists had discovered Keith's party plans. As the eight male guests were lined up to be body searched, a nude Marianne was led upstairs by two women police officers to undergo similarly humiliating treatment. In other rooms, drugs squad officers were bagging up carved pipes and ash trays for lab analysis.

Despite the initial shock, Mick must have been breathing an inner sigh of relief. He had taken nothing illegal and all his personal possessions were clean. Then he focused on the detective sergeant standing in front of him, a green velvet jacket in one hand and a phial of four white tablets in the other.

"Is this jacket yours sir?" asked the chief superintendent mildly. "Yeah," Jagger replied, "It's mine."

"So presumably these tablets are yours?"

As the realisation swept over him, Mick's first reaction was to tell the truth. He could deny all knowledge of the pills and keep himself in the clear. He knew they were Marianne's 'uppers' and that her fingerprints would be all over the bottle. On the other hand she had a reputation as a budding English rose on the verge of a brilliant singing career. If she took the rap she might be finished. If he protected her, it would make little difference to his career.

"I said: 'Are these tablets yours Mr Jagger?'" The senior officer's question was repeated a little louder ...

"Yeah," said Mick. "They're mine."

That summer the press had a feeding frenzy on the most sensational drugs bust in British pop history. At one point Mick and Keith were even, briefly, sent to prison and a picture of Jagger in handcuffs went around the world. Some of the unprintable rumours were, however, completely untrue – like the one that had Mick making love orally to Marianne using a Mars Bar at the moment the police stormed in.

Mick's libel action was in tatters, his immediate recording and touring plans were torn up and he could look forward to new outbreaks of vindictiveness from the British Establishment. He also had a criminal record which would hang like a millstone around his neck for years.

All for helping a lady in distress. Just like a perfect English gentleman.

DONALD CROWHURST

Donald Crowhurst was a man with a dream. It was to win a round-the-world yacht race in the face of competition from the most accomplished sailors of the day. Not only did he want that victory, he needed it. The prize money was earmarked to pay off creditors before he even left dry land.

But Crowhurst woefully underestimated the abilities of his vessel and his own talents of seamanship. When he realised he would not win the race which he had started with such high expectations, he set upon an outrageous course in unchartered waters. He took short cuts, gave false radio readings to race officials and maintained a bogus log book containing details of a journey he was not in fact taking. In short, he was a cheat.

Born in India in 1932 to a railway superintendent and a schoolteacher, Crowhurst returned to Britain at the age of fifteen and lived in Reading, Berkshire. He began careers in the Royal Air Force and the Army but left both under a cloud. His RAF days ended when a prank, during which he rode a motorcycle through a barrack room, went wrong. Later he was compelled to resign from the Army after being caught trying to steal a car.

In civilian life he found a niche as an electronics engineer, got married and began a consuming passion for sailing. He even invented a radio direction-finding device for sailing boats which he christened the *Navicator*. The idea was finally taken up by Pye Radio.

After that he turned his attentions to circumnavigating the world. Inspired by the success of Sir Francis Chichester who sailed single-handedly around the world in 1967, Crowhurst set his sights on the Golden Globe race, sponsored by the *Sunday Times*.

With a specially-built trimaran called *Teignmouth Electron*, he was determined to sail his way into the record books. The first hint of the difficulties he would encounter came when he skippered his boat from a yard in Norfolk to Devon. Instead of taking three days, the trip took two weeks. If he was alarmed by the excessive vibration suffered by his craft when it got up to speed, he cast his doubts to the back of his mind.

It left him little more than a fortnight to prepare for his epic voyage. It wasn't enough time to repair the leaky hatch covers. In his haste to beat the race deadline for entrants on 31 October 1968 he left a valuable box of spares on the quayside, not to mention piping to pump out the flooded hatches.

Crowhurst was plagued with mishap upon disaster as he progressed at a painfully slow pace. His biggest problem was to keep out water. Soon he was forced to revise his early estimates that it would take him a mere 243 days to complete the course. He could have and should have turned back. But foolish pride together with lingering ambition and the need for money made him go on in the face of mounting odds.

Within six weeks he began to complete a second, false log book glamourising his pace. He stopped radio contact with race organisers for months at a time to maintain his cover.

He even put ashore in Argentina to make some repairs, strictly against the rules of the event. This misdeamenour wasn't discovered until much later.

Instead of rounding the treacherous Cape Horn, Crowhurst lingered in the South Atlantic before doubling back on himself, monitoring the progress of his rivals on radio.

Robin Knox-Johnston was in the lead position set to scoop the Golden Globe as first past the post. But the £5,000 prize money for the fastest competitor was still up for grabs as all the yachts had set sail on different dates. Crowhurst pitched himself back into the race when the second-placed Nigel Tetley was homeward bound.

Suddenly, he realised that if he won, his log books would be scrutinised and his falsifications would shine out. He decided to settle as runner up to the first two genuine competitors, happy that it would bring him valuable kudos.

But disaster struck when Nigel Tetley was forced to abandon his sinking boat 1,200 miles from home. Donald Crowhurst could not help but win the first prize for the fastest passage – at least until the judges surveyed his concocted log books.

Crowhurst was acutely aware of the shame and dishonour that would follow. His feelings of guilt were compounded when congratulatory messages began pouring across the radio waves. It was then that his nerve broke and his fragile emotions lay in tatters. Together with the loneliness of life on the open sea which he had endured for nearly seven months, it was enough to drive him mad.

Entries in his log book which were later found and examined prove his agitated state of mind in those last few months. The final entry in the log was on 1 July 1969 at 11.20 am. No one knows precisely what happened to the tortured Crowhurst. It is thought he jumped overboard to meet a watery end in the Sargasso Sea, close to the Caribbean. He was probably clutching the bogus log book which would have illustrated his deception beyond all doubt. His body was never recovered.

Nine days later the Royal Mail ship Picardy found the *Teignmouth Electron* floating in the Atlantic. Aboard, crewmen found three log books, plenty of food and fresh water but no sign of sailor Crowhurst.

The news was hailed as a tragedy at home. But doubts had already been raised by chairman of the race judges, Sir Francis Chichester, about Crowhurst's apparent bursts of incredible speed and his long lapses of radio silence.

It was enough to put two *Sunday Times* reporters, Nicholas Tomalin and Ron Hall, on the trail of a scandal. They probed the log books and pieced together the sad story of Donald Crowhurst's blighted bid for fame.

The news of the fraud sent shock waves through

the world of sailing, hitherto known for its good repute and high codes of ethics. Still, there were many who stopped short of outright condemnation out of respect for the man who paid the ultimate price for his sham.

Robin Knox-Johnston, who finally won both the Golden Globe trophy and the prize for the fastest passage, handed over the cash to an appeal fund for Crowhurst's wife and four children. "None of us should judge him too harshly," the victorious sailor remarked.

In the end, no one judged Crowhurst's shoddy action more harshly than he did himself.

JACKIE AND
ARISTOTLE ONASSIS

They were the two most powerful family dynasties in the world. On the one side the Kennedys, wealthy and with untold political influence. On the other the Onassises, with their unrivalled multibillion dollar shipping interests. Each family was used to getting its way. When they were linked through marriage, the chemistry was always going to be explosive.

So when Aristotle Onassis (Aristo to his friends) wed John F. Kennedy's widow Jackie on 20 October 1968, gossip columnists around the world rubbed their hands with glee and waited for the sparks to fly. This was a marriage scandalised from the moment it was made. Even when it ended with Aristo's death in March 1975, the slanging match over the will dragged on for many months.

Onassis fell for Jackie after the acrimonious break-up of two earlier relationships. He'd married his first wife, Athina Livanos, in 1946 when he was 40 and she was a seventeen-year-old schoolgirl. The couple had two children, Alexander and Christina, but their union ended inside thirteen years. Athina discovered Aristo making love to opera singer Maria Callas aboard the tycoon's yacht, the *Christina*, during a Mediterranean cruise.

If Maria thought she was being wooed as the new

Mrs Onassis, she was sorely disappointed. Aristotle grew tired of her, and he loathed opera. When they argued over his plan to build her a career in the movies, it was the last straw. Quietly, Aristo dropped her. He'd already seen the new woman of his dreams in the shape of Jacqueline Bouvier Kennedy, wife of the US President.

Onassis and Jackie first met in the summer of 1958 when he invited her and her husband aboard the *Christina* in Monte Carlo harbour. JFK was then still a Massachusetts senator and he jumped at the chance of meeting and talking with Winston Churchill, another of Aristo's guests. It left Onassis free to escort Jackie around his vessel. "There's something provocative about that lady," he told friends later. "She's got a carnal soul."

By 1963 the friendship between the two families had evolved into something approaching intimacy. So much so that when Jackie's third child Patrick survived only a few days after birth, it was Aristotle who ventured the idea of an Aegean cruise to help her beat depression. John Kennedy was reluctant. He was a year away from a Presidential election and he didn't much like the thought of Jackie mixing so publicly with a man who just a few years earlier had been indicted for fraud by a federal grand jury. He ordered his Under-Secretary of Commerce, Franklin D.Roosevelt Jr., and Roosevelt's wife to accompany her. Jackie's sister Lee was also in the party.

In Onassis's eyes, the cruise was a fabulous success. He stocked the *Christina* with the finest champagne, caviar and lobsters, provided a complete dance orchestra and even employed a couple of hairdressers and a masseuse. At first he kept a discreet distance from the Kennedy party but when they arrived off the Turkish coast at Izmir, Jackie demanded that her host give her a personal tour of his birthplace. Soon newspapers around the globe were carrying pictures of a laughing Jackie rambling around Izmir with Aristo or sunbathing alone with him on some secluded beach.

Back in the US, John Kennedy was furious. He reminded Jackie of the forthcoming election and the need for the President and his wife to avoid even the faintest whiff of scandal. But though he bluntly ordered her to come home, she refused. The only firm promise he could wring out of her was that she would definitely accompany him on his vote-canvassing tour of Texas in the autumn.

True to her word, Jackie was sitting at his side as the Presidential car motored through downtown Dallas. And when the assassin's bullets thundered into JFK's brain on 22 November 1963, it was she who tried to clutch him to her arms.

Onassis was one of the few outsiders invited to attend the President's funeral. Gradually, in the months that followed, he began courting Jackie through a series of trysts on both sides of the Atlantic. At one of these meetings he even took the unprecedented step of ordering staff at his Paris home on the Avenue Foch to stay in their rooms. Aristo cooked and served dinner himself.

The affair remained secret, partly because it seemed so unlikely. After five years, Jackie accepted Aristotle's marriage proposal on the understanding the ceremony was delayed until after November's Presidential election. Her brother-in-law Robert, hot favourite to win, had pleaded for the delay warning Jackie: "Do you realise that this could cost me five states?"

In August Jackie's brother-in-law Teddy Kennedy arrived in Greece to negotiate her marriage contract. The deal was for Jackie to get a one-off cash settlement of $1.5 million: the price of her agreement to waive any additional claims against the Onassis empire. (Later Jackie's American lawyers would succeed in boosting that figure massively.)

In the event, the marriage was brought forward to 15 October after news leaked to the *Boston Herald-Traveler*. Aristo and Jackie were married at 5.15pm in the Church of the Little Virgin, a tiny Greek Orthodox chapel on the Ionian isle of Skorpios. The press had little chance of sneaking in. Aristo owned the entire island and managed to get his old friends in Greece's military junta to send along a couple of warships for good measure.

Yet hardly had the flower petals and rice been swept away than the tone of the troubled union was set. Onassis left his honeymoon to close business deals and Jackie returned to New York where she could be nearer her children John and Caroline. There was also the obvious attraction of Manhattan, particularly its fashion shops and department stores.

Observers believe Jackie spent a million dollars of Aristo's money in their first twelve months of marriage. At first he shrugged off her shop-till-you-drop philosophy saying: "There's nothing strange in the fact that my wife spends large sums of money. Think how people would react if Mrs Onassis wore the same dresses for two years." Crudely, he would also boast of their exciting sex life: "Five times a night! She surpasses all the other women I've ever known."

But when the spending spree showed no sign of ending, Aristo's frustration began to show through. "What does she do with all these clothes?" he asked friends. "I never see her in anything but jeans." Onassis decided to curb his wife's spending, slicing a third off her allowance and shifting the account to Monte Carlo where it was easier to monitor.

The marriage troubles were only just beginning. In 1970 a letter from Jackie to her close friend Roswell Gilpatric was published in America. Jackie had written it during her so-called honeymoon with Aristo and it was a damning revelation of her true feelings.

"Dearest Ros, I would have told you before I left but then everything happened so much more quickly than I'd planned. I saw somewhere what you had said and I was very touched – dear Ros – I hope you know all you were and are and ever will be to me. With my love, Jackie."

Aristotle was livid. "My God, what a fool I've made of myself," he told friends. In a tit-for-tat move he rang up his old flame Maria Callas and made a point of dining with her very publicly at Maxim's restaurant in Paris. Jackie responded to this taunt by flying to Paris the next day and demanding to eat at the very same table.

Three years later Aristo's patience finally snapped. He discovered Jackie had spent $300,000 on lawyers' fees after accusing a photographer of invading her privacy. The net result of the case was that the photographer concerned, Ron Galella, was prohibited from going closer than seven metres to her. It was all unbelievably pointless to Onassis's eyes and he decided it was symptomatic of the way his marriage would shape up in future. He instructed one of America's most feared divorce lawyers, Roy Cohn and sat back to await events.

But by now the magic touch with which Onassis seemed gifted in the Sixties had begun to desert him. He was devastated at the death of his son Alexander in a plane crash in 1973 and found himself at odds with Christina over her choice of a husband, US property magnate Joseph Bolker, a man 29 years her senior.

Aristo also suffered a run of damaging business reverses, culminating in the takeover of his beloved Olympic Airways by the Greek government. This had a knock-on effect on his health so that by 1975 he was almost completely incapacitated. A wasting disease that afflicted him was so rampant it meant his eyelids had to be taped open.

Onassis died in Paris on 15 March, aged 69, following an attack of bronchial pneumonia.

Christina was at his bedside and it was she who took charge of the funeral arrangements and the task of ferrying his body back to Skorpios. On arrival at Greece's Aktion air base she and Jackie put on a show of unity, walking arm in arm across the tarmac, both dressed all in black.

But as the cortege headed for the ferry, onlookers watched in amazement as Christina halted the lead car and stormed out to take a seat in the one behind. It was later rumoured that this was the precise moment at which Teddy Kennedy had started talking about the will. What, he wondered, was in it for Jackie?

The answer was $37 million, but only after some high-powered 'horse-trading' in which Jackie's lawyers waged an eighteen-month war of attrition to challenge the will. In return, Jackie waived her annuity, her 25% share in the Onassis yacht and her claim on part of Skorpios.

Christina fought her all the way, until her death from a drugs overdose in November 1988. And when Jackie herself succumbed to cancer in May 1994, she went to her grave knowing that she had never been forgiven by the Onassis clan.

EDWARD KENNEDY

Edgartown is a pretty New England town, beloved of tourists, fishermen and yachtsmen. It is also beloved of the rich and famous who pass through it on their way to the island of Martha's Vineyard, a brief ferry ride offshore. On 19 July 1969 Edgartown's police chief, Jim Dominick Arena, sat opposite one of the most famous of the island's visitors, Senator Edward Kennedy, while he made a written statement. Arena read it stunned:

"On 18 July 1969, at approximately 11.15pm on Chappaquiddick Island, Martha's Vineyard, I was driving my car on Main Street on my way to get the ferry back to Edgartown. I was unfamiliar with the road and turned onto Dyke Road instead of bearing left on Main Street. After proceeding for approximately half a mile on Dyke Road I descended a hill and came upon a narrow bridge.

"There was one passenger with me, Miss Kopechne, a former secretary of my brother Robert Kennedy. The car turned over and sank into the water and landed with the roof resting on the bottom. I attempted to open the door and window of the car but have no recollection of how I got out of the car. I came to the surface and then repeatedly dove down to the car in an attempt to see if the passenger was still in the car. I was unsuccessful in the attempt. I was exhausted and in a state of shock.

"I recall walking back to where my friends were

Edward Kennedy wearing a neck brace after his car crash.

eating. There was a car in front of the cottage and I climbed into the back seat. I then asked for someone to bring me back to Edgartown. I remember walking around for a period of time and then going back to my hotel room. When I fully realised what had happened this morning I immediately contacted the police."

The statement (and other prevaricating speeches he was yet to make) was such a tissue of half-truths that it shocked police chief Arena. It also gave the American public an insight into the mind, emotions and morals of a man who, following the assassination of his brothers John and Robert, would almost certainly have become President of the United States of America. That dream was ended by his actions on Chappaquiddick.

On 18 July the 37-year-old Edward Kennedy completed a day's sailing, called in to the Edgartown Harbour hotel where he had a room, downed a beer or two and was joined by a party of friends, including his cousin Joe Gargan and his lawyer Paul Markham. Apart from the hotel room, Kennedy had rented a secluded cottage on the islet of Chappaquiddick, part of the larger island of Martha's Vineyard. There, after a brief ferry ride from Edgartown, Kennedy and his two male friends were joined by three other men and six young women. There was to be party ...

The barbecue party seemed set to be an all-night affair. Yet after only three hours Mary Jo Kopechne left the cottage with Teddy Kennedy, who drove off with her into the night in his 1967 black Oldsmobile.

Kennedy claimed that he was taking Mary Jo to catch a midnight ferry back to her Edgartown hotel. Half way across the island of Chappaquiddick, however, he failed to take an obvious left turn into Main Street and instead turned right down a narrow lane leading to the 85ft long Dyke Bridge. As he crossed it, his car skidded over the edge and landed upside down in eight feet of water.

After Teddy Kennedy scrambled clear, and after making his various attempts to reach the drowning Mary Jo, Teddy Kennedy went through all the actions of a coward trying to cover up a shameful act.

He rested for about fifteen minutes before heading back along the lane towards the cottage. After a couple of hundred yards he passed another house but did not stop to use the telephone and raise the alarm. At this time, it was later discovered, Mary Jo might still have been alive in a bubble of air inside the car.

Upon reaching the cottage, cold and drenched, Kennedy remained outside and called for his two friends, Gargan and Markham, to join him. They did not alert any of Mary Jo's friends; instead the threesome drove secretly back to the scene of the accident. There they again made unsuccessful dives to try to reach the girl before driving off to the ferry wharf overlooking the channel to Edgartown.

On the water's edge, a sobbing Kennedy warned his friends to keep the accident a secret from the other guests. Then, instead of summoning a ferryman by public phone, he inexplicably dived into the water and swam across to the mainland. There he quietly entered his hotel and went to his room.

In the morning, Gargan and Markham came across on an early ferry. And only then – at least ten hours after the crash – did Kennedy report the incident. Police chief Jim Arena, who by then had already been notified of the wrecked car and had raced across the channel to investigate, stared dumbfounded as he read the statement of half-truths dictated by the senator for Massachusetts.

The Kennedy clan's hot-shot lawyers took up the case. Teddy was charged with leaving the scene of an accident, but his guilty plea saved him the shame of giving evidence at the hearing, where he was given a three-month sentence – suspended.

It did not, however, silence the growing clamour by press and public about what was so obviously a cover-up. So, as the high point of an elaborate public relations exercise, Kennedy went on nationwide television to make a long and detailed – yet still evasive and inconclusive – statement about his actions on the night of 18 July in Chappaquiddick. Part of it ran thus:

"Miss Mary Jo Kopechne ... was such a gentle, kind and idealistic person, all of us tried to help her feel she had a home with the Kennedy family. There is no truth whatsoever to the widely circulated suspicions of immoral conduct that have been levelled at my behaviour and hers regarding that evening. There has never been a private relationship between us of any kind ... Nor was I driving under the influence of liquor."

Edward Kennedy stumbled on in his televised attempt to explain his strange actions after his Oldsmobile crashed into the water off Dyke Bridge:

"All kinds of scrambled thoughts – all of them confused, some of them irrational, many of which I cannot recall and some of which I would not have entertained under normal circumstances – went through my mind during this period. They were reflected in the various, inexplicable, inconsistent and inconclusive things I said and did, including such things as whether the girl might still be alive outside of that immediate area, whether some awful curse did actually hang over all the Kennedys, whether there was some justifiable reason for me to doubt what had happened and to delay my report, whether somehow the awful weight of this incredible incident might in some way pass from my shoulders.

"I was overcome, I'm frank to say, by a jumble of emotions: grief, fear, doubt, exhaustion, panic, confusion and shock ..."

So it went on, ending with a whining appeal to be allowed to continue his political ambitions and remain Senator for Massachusetts: "I seek your advice and opinion; I seek your prayers."

The answer was swift. *Life* magazine summed it up: "He was simply hustling heartstrings, using words, cashing in on the family credibility."

Over the years that followed, Edward Kennedy tried again and again to re-establish himself as the last Kennedy champion of the Democratic cause. But the name Mary Jo Kopechne was raised so often in the press that he was generally forced to withdraw – as silently and as ignominiously as he had withdrawn from the scene of the death at Dyke Bridge. Teddy Kennedy languished in a political pool bounded by bouts of boozing and womanising. His hopes of ultimate power had withered and died with the ghost of Mary Jo Kopechne.

WATERGATE

It started as a trickle and ended as a flood. Watergate was the name of it, and it became the greatest scandal in the history of the United States of America. From insignificant beginnings, it grew to proportions that eventually put paid to the President himself.

At 12.45am on the night of 17 June 1972, security guard Frank Wills uncovered a burglary at the Watergate office complex on the bank of the Potomac River in Washington. Wills, a 24-year-old college drop-out, first spotted a length of adhesive tape stretched across the lock of a door in the basement. Removing it, the door then locked shut, and Wills continued on his rounds.

An hour later, however, he returned to the same spot and found that the tape had been replaced with a fresh strip. Suddenly he realised that someone had broken in – and was probably still somewhere inside the building.

Wills phoned the police and soon a three-man patrol was searching the building. They found similar lengths of tape on doors on the sixth floor.

Drawing their guns, the cops crept into one office where they saw a shadowy figure crouching behind a desk.

"Come out!" one policeman shouted. "And keep your hands in the air."

To their surprise, not one but five burglars stepped

Disgraced President Richard Nixon was forced out of office.

out from behind partitions and filing cabinets. They were wearing blue rubber gloves and were carrying cameras and sophisticated bugging equipment. After giving false names, all five were arrested and led through the complex to the adjoining Watergate Hotel, where two of the men had room keys. On the burglars and in their rooms, police found more than $5,000, mainly in unused hundred-dollar bills. They also found address books containing the telephone numbers of senior White House staff. The fuse of the Watergate scandal had been lit ...

The burglars eventually gave police their real names and they all appeared in Washington's Superior Court that same day. They were: James W. McCord, a former CIA officer; Virgilio Gonzalez, a locksmith and ex-CIA agent; Eugenio Martinez, also a Cuban exile and ex-CIA contact; Frank Sturgis, a former US Marine, now a soldier of fortune; and Bernard Barker, another CIA agent. In court, all gave their occupations as 'anti-communists'.

The story at first failed to make big headlines. President Richard Milhous Nixon was in the middle of a re-election campaign. He and his campaign manager, Attorney General John Mitchell, were quick to disown the burglars. The press and public swallowed the story and Nixon was duly voted in for another term.

Six months later, however, two journalists on *The Washington Post*, who refused to let the story rest, discovered that $114,000 of 'campaign contributions' had been paid into burglar Barker's bank account shortly before the break-in. The cash was from the Campaign For The Re-election Of President Nixon – known as CREEP for short.

It transpired that the five burglars were part of a team who called themselves 'the plumbers'. More properly known as the White House Special Investigations Unit, their job was to rifle through the files of Nixon's Democratic rivals, harass them and invent scandals about them.

This scandal, however, was about to rebound on 'the plumbers' in a big way.

The Washington Post discovered that the investigation unit was led by two White House staffers: G. Gordon Liddy, a former district attorney, and Howard Hunt, a CIA officer. Both men had been watching the Watergate burglary from the safety of an adjoining building. But even they were not the top guns in the dirty-tricks campaign. They took their orders directly from President Nixon's chief domestic advisor, John Ehrlichman.

On 8 January 1973 the burglary trial opened with two additional defendants, Liddy and Hunt. All were found guilty, and sentences were deferred. This was a ploy by District Court Chief Judge John Sirica to make the accused sweat in fear of threatened heavy sentences. (When the sentences were eventually announced, they were disproportionate to the crimes – some as high as 30 years in jail – although they were later drastically reduced.)

The judge's tactics paid off. McCord was the first to crack, claiming that senior White House officials had been involved in the break-in and subsequent cover-up.

Nixon's legal counsel John Dean was named. Called before a Senate investigative committee twelve months after the Watergate burglary, he admitted discussions with the President over the raising of $1million for the Watergate 'plumbers'. One by one, other reluctant witnesses were called from the White House to give evidence about the workings of CREEP and other subversive groups.

With the press also digging deeper into these murky political waters, a picture slowly emerged of unauthorised wire taps, illegal campaign contributions, blackmail, smear tactics and theft. All of these were commonplace inside the Nixon administration. The web of deceit and lies spread like a cancer over the White House.

President Nixon himself continued to claim that he had had no prior knowledge of the Watergate break-in. Nor had he any knowledge of a cover-up. Nor did he authorise the subsequent conspiracy to pervert the course of justice.

Then, on 16 July 1973, a minor member of the White House security staff casually dropped the bombshell that was to expose President Nixon's lies. Alexander Butterfield, under routine questioning before the Senate committee, revealed that every conversation that took place within the President's Oval Office of the White House was tape-recorded.

Those recording would prove once and for all what Nixon's response had been when told of the arrest of the Watergate burglars. The President was ordered to hand over the tapes.

For four months, Nixon fought to retain the recordings. He claimed 'executive privilege', asserting that many secret matters of state would become public along with the Watergate references. He argued that to comply would 'unquestionably destroy any vestige of confidentiality of presidential communications'. Pleadingly, during one nationally televised speech, he said:

"I am not a crook ..."

But he was. The tapes eventually became part of the public record, revealing Richard Nixon to be a foul-mouthed, vindictive man who had abused the trust of the entire nation. The catchphrase 'expletive deleted' became a lingual joke around the world – for it was the most common phrase in the transcripts of those tapes which the reluctant President had handed over.

Investigations surrounding the workings of CREEP also revealed evidence of laundering of campaign money. Eight corporations pleaded guilty to charges of adding illegal campaign contributions to Nixon's coffers.

Irregularities were also found in the President's tax affairs, and he was ordered to repay more than half-a-million dollars in back taxes. In addition, he had used $20 million of taxpayers' money to improve his homes in Florida and California.

By June 1974, with the walls now starting to tumble around him, Nixon became a prisoner inside the White House, besieged by an angry Congress, judiciary and the media. Unable to sleep, he became distrustful of even the few loyal aides who were trying to defend him to the end.

The following month, John Ehrlichman and other White House 'plumbers' were found guilty of conspiracy. Two weeks later the Supreme Court ruled unanimously that Nixon had no choice but to surrender 64 remaining tapes from the Oval Office. Finally, on 5 August, he was forced to hand over a final three tapes – which clearly proved him to have instigated attempts to gag the FBI in their attempts to investigate Watergate.

On the evening of 7 August he took his family for a last trip on the presidential boat up the Potomac River, on the banks of which stood the Watergate building. Aboard, he began sobbing – and ended up beating his head against the bulwarks and the carpet. Vice-President Gerald Ford was warned that very night that he should be ready to take power.

The end came two days later, on 9 August 1974. Warned that he would be impeached unless he resigned, Richard Nixon made an emotional farewell speech to his staff at the White House. Many wept openly.

In the nearest to an apology that President Nixon ever made, he told the nation in a televised speech:

"I regret deeply any injuries that may have been done in the course of events that led to this decision ... I would only say that if some of my judgments were wrong – and some were wrong – they were made in what I believed at the time to be the best interest of the nation."

The President of the United States then boarded a helicopter on the White House lawns and fled from office to his Californian seaside retreat. The greatest scandal ever to afflict the world's most powerful nation had painfully drawn to an end.

JOHN STONEHOUSE

The charming, good looking Englishman strolled casually up to the Miami Beach office of the luxurious Fontainbleau Hotel. The receptionist in charge, 65-year-old Mrs Helen Fleming, was more than willing to pass the time of day with him. Business was quiet and they were able to have a long, uninterrupted conversation.

Before he left, the gentleman mentioned that his name was John Stonehouse and that he was going for a swim. He wished her good day and she watched as he strolled casually down to the thundering surf, seemingly just another Brit soaking up the Florida sun.

Hours later his clothes were found in a neat pile on the sand. Of John Stonehouse there was no trace.

So began one of the most audacious deceptions of the 20th century. Yet it proved much more than an elaborate con trick.

Stonehouse was a Labour Member of the British Parliament with personal debts of around £375,000. His business empire lay in tatters and his personal life – he was attempting to keep both a wife and mistress in tow – was a constant strain. His attempt to drag himself out of the mire by apparently vanishing off the face of the earth was nothing short of a gigantic political scandal.

And yet when he took his seat in the House of Commons in 1957 Stonehouse had seemed destined

Runaway John Stonehouse with loyal lover Sheila
Buckley.

for the very top. After serving his apprenticeship on the backbenches he was talent-spotted by Harold Wilson and put on the fast track to promotion.

During the Wilson years, he rose from Aviation Minister and Technology Minister to become Postmaster General. As a privy counsellor, he was entitled to be known as the Right Honourable John Stonehouse. And he was so close to the PM that Wilson lent him his private holiday home on the Scilly Isles. He was even tipped as the PM's successor.

When Labour was booted out by the electorate in 1970, Stonehouse decided he could not accept either the comparative anonymity or the reduced salary of life on the Commons backbenches. He began pumping money into a web of companies, including a merchant bank, in a bid to make his fortune.

Over the next four years not one of them returned a decent profit. Stonehouse resorted to the oldest trick in the book – switching funds between them to satisfy investors and auditors that all was well.

In his heart, he probably knew it couldn't last, and in early 1974 he got wind that Department of Trade investigators were taking an interest in his companies. Even the political 'old boy' network couldn't help him now and he resolved to take desperate measures in a bid to avoid exposure. He disliked the idea of spending the rest of his life on the run so there was only one thing for it ... he would have to 'die'.

Stonehouse decided that only one person should share his secret: his divorced mistress and secretary Sheila Buckley, then 28. The aim would be for them to live together in New Zealand, living off whatever money he could smuggle out from the wreckage of his businesses. There was only one snag: he had to have a new identity.

To get round this Stonehouse used a technique described by thriller writer Frederick Forsyth in his classic *The Day of the Jackal*. He first tricked a hospital in his Walsall, Staffordshire, constituency to release personal details on two men of his own age who had died recently – Donald Mildoon and Joseph Markham.

The 48-year-old MP then obtained copies of their birth certificates and, believing Markham's background was closest to his own, applied for a passport in that man's name. He obtained photo-booth shots of himself wearing glasses and smiling and on the back forged the counter-signature of an MP he knew to be dying of cancer, Neil McBride.

The application was rubber-stamped at the Passport Office and on 2 August 1974 Stonehouse picked up his new passport. He now had a duel identity and could switch his name whenever necessary.

Now came the second part of his plan. Over the next three months, he opened 27 accounts in his own name and a further nine in the names of Markham or Mildoon. A Swiss bank received one huge cheque credited to Mr Markham while further amounts were quietly channelled via a London account to the Bank of New South Wales.

Numerous credit cards were set up in Markham's

name using an anonymous address at a downmarket London hotel. He even set up a company to help his cover story: 'J.A.Markham, export-import consultant'. The only exports it handled were cash and the only customer was Stonehouse.

After a dummy run to the US, Stonehouse was ready for the real thing. He left London for Miami on 19 November 1974 with Jim Charlton, deputy chairman of one of his companies. When he failed to return from his swimming trip the following day there seemed little doubt that he had drowned. The message flashed from Miami Beach Police Department to New Scotland Yard read: 'John Stonehouse Presumed Dead.'

Of course they were wrong. After dumping his clothes the MP had raced up the beach to a ramshackle building where he had hidden a suitcase containing new clothes, cash and false identity papers. He took a taxi to the airport, flew to Hawaii via San Fransisco and then called Sheila Buckley to tell her their scheme had worked like a dream.

But the optimism was premature. Stonehouse arrived in Australia and was soon switching cash from a bank account in Melbourne, held under the name of Mildoon, to one in New Zealand belonging to Joseph Markham. The amounts were more than enough to raise the suspicions of bank officials and soon the police were called in. A tail was put on Stonehouse who, by 10 December, was beavering away daily, transferring funds between a string of banks. The only brief respite came with a flight to Copenhagen for a tryst with Sheila Buckley.

The net seemed to be closing, yet Stonehouse might still have bluffed his way out had it not been for an unfortunate twist of fate.

That autumn police across Australia had been briefed to look out for Lord Lucan, the English peer who had disappeared after murdering his family nanny. When Victoria State Police asked Scotland Yard for more pictures of Lucan they received some of John Stonehouse too. The missing MP bore a remarkable resemblance to Joseph Markham.

Stonehouse was arrested on Christmas Eve 1974. At first he laughed off the questions about his false identity but a love-note from Sheila Buckley found in his jacket ended the pretence. It read: "Dear Dum Dums (her pet nickname for her lover). Do miss you. So lonely. Shall wait forever for you."

Both Sheila and Stonehouse's 45-year-old wife Barbara flew to Australia to be at his side. Barbara quickly returned to the UK to file divorce papers but Sheila stayed on until his extradition in July 1975.

After a 68-day trial the disgraced politician was found guilty on eighteen counts of theft, forgery and fraud. He was given a seven-year sentence. His mistress got two years, suspended, for aiding and abetting him.

The judge's comments at the end of the trial, that Stonehouse was an 'extremely persuasive, deceitful and ambitious man', mattered little to Sheila Buckley. She waited for him for three years – and through two heart attacks suffered in prison – to take back a bankrupt and seriously ill man.

They married in secret in 1981 and for the next few years the former MP tried to switch into thriller writing. He didn't make it big as an author. Perhaps his imagination couldn't compete with the astonishing exploits of the real John Stonehouse.

He died, aged 62, in 1989. Later Sheila said of him:

"I've never met a man like him. John was gentle with everybody and, in particular, with me. I'll miss him forever."

IMELDA MARCOS

Imelda Romualdez was a poor, barefoot child who wore hand-me-down clothes and faced a bleak future in the poverty-stricken Philippines. During the Japanese occupation in World War II, her family lost all of its possessions, except for one necklace of very poor diamonds which they sold off one stone at a time. As a teenager, the best Imelda was told to expect was a menial job in a bank where one of her relatives could perhaps find her a vacancy.

There was one thing Imelda did have going for her, however. As a teenager, she flowered into ravishing womanhood, with classic Asian good looks that she quickly realised would be a greater asset to her than her family or her education. Coupled with this was a voracious greed born, said those closest to her, out of her impoverished childhood.

Beauty and greed combined to trap her a fabulous prize: a husband who was a young senator in the Philippines government. His name was Ferdinand Marcos.

Wed in 1954, the couple were a formidable political team. They were the most glamorous political double-act the Philippines had ever witnessed, and they inspired the same sort of excitement as John Kennedy and his wife Jacqueline aroused in the United States.

In 1965 Marcos, with his beautiful consort by his side, was voted into the presidency – and Imelda took to the role with a fervour even her energetic husband could not match as she drew her strength from the vast crowds she attracted.

The couple were to rule the islands with an iron fist for 21 years. Their honeymoon with the voters, however, did not last that long. In 1972 Marcos realised that he was likely to lose the next election for his third term of office. He declared martial law.

Seldom was the adage "absolute power corrupts absolutely" proven more true than when Imelda Marcos found herself the consort of the absolute ruler of the Philippines. She became more regal than a queen. Champagne, caviar, limousines and helicopters were considered *de rigeur*. Her greed, gluttony and selfishness knew no bounds. While the nation's economy floundered, she wasted millions on clothes. The first lady would even instruct her ladies-in-waiting what to wear on a particular day.

She chartered a plane to import a load of sand from Australia because the beach bordering her summer estate was not white enough. She travelled the world on multimillion-dollar shopping expeditions, accompanied by retinues of aides. She stayed only in the presidential suites of the most expensive hotels, where there was a standing instruction for $1,000 of fresh flowers to be placed in her rooms nightly. Whenever she landed at Manila airport, all air traffic was halted as welcoming parties flooded onto the runway.

Meanwhile, the peasants of the Philippines grew poorer. While her former supporters starved and

Big-spender: Imelda Marcos's wardrobe of designer shoes.

babies in the hospitals went without vital medicines, Imelda's pet dog wore a diamond collar.

In 1979 Imelda and Ferdinand celebrated their 25th wedding anniversary. For the occasion, she refurbished their Malacanang Palace at a cost of several millions. She bought a silver carriage complete with eight white horses, hired trumpeters in full regalia to herald the arrival of guests and constructed a theatre-like chapel in the palace hall. Imelda wore a white wedding gown with a rosary of diamonds. The price tag: $5 million.

Despite the exorbitant celebration of their love, the Marcos couple were by now barely on speaking terms with one another. Ferdinand had taken a mistress and, when tipped off about her, Imelda had her thrown out of the country. The mistress, however, had recorded some of their lovemaking sessions, and these tapes were distributed among the Marcos's political enemies. Imelda was humiliated and infuriated.

She sated her rage by going on still wider and wilder spending sprees. In one 1983 trip to Rome and New York, she spent $5 million in just 90 days – including $12,000 on bath towels and more than $3 million on a Michelangelo painting. On another trip to New York, she bought buildings on Wall Street, Madison Avenue and Fifth Avenue, plus homes in New Jersey and Long Island.

It all had to end, of course, although the Marcos duo hung on to power for as long as they could.

Then, in August 1983, as Ferdinand's health

deteriorated and Imelda meddled more and more in affairs of state, their toughest political opponent, Ninoy Aquino, returned to the Philippines after several years of exile in the US. As he stepped off the plane at Manila airport, he was shot dead.

Gradually, the Marcos dynasty's strongest ally, the US government, could no longer defend the pair's excesses.

There was also a sustained campaign of protest, demonstration and insurrection at home. Ferdinand reacted in 1986 by calling a snap election; but this time he had seriously misjudged the mood of the country.

Aquino's widow, Corazan, stood against the president. Imelda dismissed her as "a woman without facial make-up" and "a puppet of the communists". Meanwhile, Ferdinand tried to buy victory with rigged polling stations.

Corazan Aquino swept to power – yet Marcos still declared himself the winner. Ferdinand and Imelda refused to budge from their palace, and the country was plunged into near-revolution. Finally, following some no-nonsense ultimatums from the US, the couple realised that their time was up. They fled to exile in Hawaii.

The new regime took over the fabulous Malacanang Palace. There, beneath Imelda's wood-panelled bedroom, they found a 5,000 square-feet basement containing: 2,700 pairs of shoes, 1,200 designer gowns, 500 black brassieres and 35 racks of fur coats.

But there were worse discoveries to come; with the help of her husband, Imelda had stolen an estimated $5 billion from the Philippines Treasury and had salted it away in bank accounts around the world.

Ferdinand Marcos died in Hawaii three years later, leaving Imelda to fight a string of court cases in an attempt to retain at least some of her hidden wealth – by then estimated at anything up to $10 billion.

JOHN DE LOREAN

As a youthful Michael J. Fox steered his futuristic car across cinema screens in the film *Back to the Future*, millions of envious schoolchildren imagined themselves in the driving seat. With its sleek lines, gull-wing doors and silver-grey finish the dream machine looked the ultimate in automobile one-upmanship.

What few film fans realised, however, was that the car's Hollywood image and its real-life road performance were worlds apart. For it was a De Lorean 12, perhaps the most unreliable, shoddy, ill-conceived, hotch-potch of a vehicle ever to be rolled off a production line.

The story of the De Lorean Motor Company is almost as bizarre as the plot of Fox's film. Its birth and rapid demise ranks as one of the biggest financial scandals ever to afflict the British taxpayer, and it is a permanent reminder to governments everywhere of the folly of throwing good money after bad.

The saga began in October 1975 when an ambitious Detroit-based automotive engineer, John De Lorean, aged 50, registered his new company with the US authorities. Born and bred in Motor City, he looked to have the skills, drive and pedigree to turn the venture into a rip-roaring success. He also realised that if he was to milk money out of customers in the blue-chip, high-performance end of the car market, creating the right image would be crucial.

Silver-tongued John De Lorean with his gull-winged silver sports car.

De Lorean began trying to raise private capital to develop and build his brainchild, the DMC-12. His team pulled in more than $6 million including a lump sum of $550,000 from the legendary TV chat show host Johnny Carson. Considering that the fund-raisers had not even a prototype to show investors, this was no mean achievement.

But it wasn't enough. The money was being pumped into the development programme as fast as it was arriving and, of course, there was De Lorean's six-figure consultancy retainer to think of. He was already enjoying the perks of a successful executive and had installed himself and his beautiful wife Cristina in a luxury New York apartment overlooking Central Park.

De Lorean acknowledged that if his dream was to reach fruition he had to attract big money into the pot. He reckoned $80 million was needed, but the problem might then be that outside investors would try to dictate his managerial policy. The idea was an anathema to him. The DMC was his baby and no one else was going to mess with it.

And so he began casting around for a state or national government prepared to offer juicy grants and low-cost loans in return for the large number of jobs DMC production would create. A queue quickly formed – Spain, Puerto Rico, Michigan, Rhode Island, Ohio, Maine, and two Canadian provinces – and it seemed Puerto Rico would close the deal. Then at the last minute the British Labour government and its Northern Ireland Development Administration,

NIDA, stepped in with an offer De Lorean could not refuse.

The package was worth $97 million comprising one third in direct grants, a further $20 million in loans (which could be turned into grants provided enough jobs were created), a $12 million low-cost loan on the lease of the Belfast factory and a direct government investment. De Lorean himself had to put up a piffling $1 million. For that he got an incredible 73% voting control.

It was no surprise then that on 3 August 1978, a little over six weeks after NIDA first made its bid, De Lorean signed the deal and sat back to bank his cheque courtesy of the British taxpayer. Everything was now in place apart from one significant detail. John De Lorean decided a little of that cash could be tucked away somewhere safe. First thing on the morning of 18 October, one of his New York executives was ordered to draw a cheque made out to a Panama-registered company's Swiss bank account. The company was called GPD Services and the cheque was for a cool $12.5 million.

GPD remains one of the great enigmas of the De Lorean scandal. It seems to have had only one employee, Mrs Marie-Denise Juhan, though according to De Lorean it was a vital part of his empire. He claimed it provided engineers and sub-contracted work to the highly-respected Lotus Cars Ltd, founded by entrepreneur Colin Chapman. True, Lotus did do most of the development work on the DMC-12, with contracts worth $24 million. But that money was paid directly by De Lorean's Northern Ireland office, not by some intangible offshore company. Incredibly, $17.76 million found its way to GPD over eighteen months. What happened to it then is pure conjecture. One thing is certain: it never got anywhere near Belfast.

Later, De Lorean's financial controller Walter Strycker recalled: "When we first heard about GPD some of us thought about the possibility that John and Chapman put their hands on the money. But just as quickly we dismissed the idea. Here John had the opportunity to make hundreds of millions with the car company. Why would he risk that before the thing had even gotten off the ground? It would be such a goddamn stupid thing to do; we just couldn't believe John would have done it."

De Lorean had promised the British government that his DMC-12 would be in pilot production by May 1980 and would hit the full production target of 30,000 vehicles per year late in 1981. It was a hopelessly ambitious timescale given that an entire factory had to be built and equipped and an unskilled labour force trained.

In fact, by October 1980, the DMC-12 was back on the drawing board. Colin Chapman had decided he liked nothing about the prototype and had begun re-designing every inch of it. De Lorean himself seemed oblivious to the impending crisis, refusing to base himself full-time in Belfast to oversee progress. The main reason for this was that he hated Northern Ireland and feared he could become an IRA target. It was a ludicrous worry. De Lorean was providing hundreds of vital jobs for Catholics in the city. Had IRA leaders threatened the plant in any way, they would have faced uproar from the very people they purported to represent.

The production delays were only part of the problem. De Lorean was somehow managing to fritter away $8 million a year on his New York headquarters, even though it had a staff of only 30. His personal 'expenses' were topping $120,000 dollars a year and his annual 'consultant's fee' was a hefty $300,000. Yet when his financial staff confronted him with the sorry figures De Lorean responded by demanding more money from the British government, now headed by the Conservative Prime Minister Margaret Thatcher.

At first he succeeded. The Northern Ireland Office gave him an extra loan of $33 million, which brought the total UK taxpayers' investment to $120,000 million with not a single car to show for it.

De Lorean was told categorically that he would get no more cash – yet within two months, in December 1980, he was demanding another $20 million as an 'inflation adjustment'. His letter to Tony Hopkins, head of the Northern Ireland Development Administration, threatened: "You owe us $20 million. If you give it to us we have enough money to finish the job properly ... it is squarely up to NIDA. If you cannot or will not provide the balance of funding you owe us we plan to shut down our operations on both sides of the Atlantic immediately."

Hopkins was in no mood to be pushed around and sent back a curt refusal. Undeterred, De Lorean then approached the Northern Ireland Department of Commerce which agreed to guarantee a $40 million loan from two commercial banks. The running total was $160 million. Still there were no cars.

Finally, on 21 January 1981 John De Lorean drove the first DMC-12 out of the factory and into the spotlight of the waiting media. It looked impressive but what the assembled journalists did not know was that it had been thrown together in a panic to meet the photocall deadline. Underneath that sleek stainless steel bodywork lay a creaking mass of badly fitting and unreliable engineering.

Typically, its performance and specifications were nothing like De Lorean had promised. It was supposed to do 32 miles per gallon; it actually did 20. It was supposed to weigh 998 kg; it actually topped 1,360. It was supposed to do 0-60 mph in 8 seconds; it actually took 10.5. It was supposed to cost customers £15,000; its actual retail price was £25,000. But the indefatigable De Lorean was unhestitating in his praise. "It's a winner," he told motoring journalists.

De Lorean's US marketing manager Dick Brown later succinctly summed up the truth: "I'll tell you what it looked like. It looked like somebody put a hand grenade in the front seat and the back seat and set them off. All the guts were out. You couldn't ride in them. You looked in the window and all the components were just stuffed in. They weren't built in, they were stuffed in. Doors wouldn't function, electronics wouldn't function. We had to re-design and re-tool some parts here just to make them work."

The design faults were embarrasingly obvious, even to the layman. One potential customer was trapped inside the car at the Cleveland motor show for an hour because the gull-wing doors refused to open. He later bought a Corvette. Another wrote to De Lorean himself saying: "When it doesn't start due to a short in the ignition switch, I am embarrassed. When the headlights don't turn off, I am embarrassed. When the signal lights don't work, I am endangered. When the fuel gauge doesn't work, I am stuck. And when the roof leaks, I get wet."

Despite all this, the car was an initial success changing hands for $5,000 above its brochure price. De Lorean celebrated by buying Cristina and himself a $3.4 million home. He also decided to float his company on the New York stock exchange, which effectively meant the British government's initial investment would be converted into shares belonging to him. It was an outrageous and arrogant act and for the first time MPs began seriously to question De Lorean's motives.

Worse, the British press caught the whiff of scandal. One by one, editors turned their investigative reporters loose on John De Lorean and the entire can of worms was soon open.

"Why," asked the *Sunday Telegraph*, "should a Panamanian-registered partnership based at PO Box 33, 1211, Geneva, Switzerland, have received on behalf of Colin Chapman's Lotus Group some $18 million from the state-aided De Lorean sports car concern?" The newspaper's probe was followed by further, damning revelations into De Lorean's business practices. The source was as good as it could possibly be – his private secretary Marian Gibson.

From now on it was all downhill for the DMC-12. Sales were plummeting as the car's design and production faults became increasingly obvious. The flotation plan folded and a financial re-structuring put forward by the British government was scrapped when it emerged that De Lorean had been arrested by the FBI for allegedly attempting to raise funds through cocaine smuggling. He was later cleared by a jury, but it was too late to save his dream.

The ailing DMC was in receivership, never to produce another of its ill-fated cars. Later an all-party committee of British MPs would describe the wasted $160 million of taxpayers' cash as 'one of the gravest cases of misuse of public resources for many years'.

ELVIS PRESLEY

One hundred thousand fans poured into town for his funeral. Over 3,000 wreaths were sent, including some from the Soviet Union and China. The city of Memphis erected a statue to its favourite son. Tens of thousands still tour Graceland, the home where he died.

Yet despite those millions of adoring fans, hundreds of hangers-on, dozens of bodyguards and a live-in lover, on the day Elvis Presley died of a massive heart attack he lay alone on his bathroom floor for more than five hours before anyone discovered his body. The date was 16 August 1977.

Elvis was The King to a rock 'n' rollin' world. But he was a sad, sick, obese wreck by the time his drug-abused body finally gave up at the age of 42.

At the end, he shut himself away in his bedroom suite, with its two television sets built into the ceiling. He would watch pornographic movies, some of which he had made himself while watching friends indulge in sex acts through two-way mirrors. He had also become obsessed with guns, shooting out the TV screens if he didn't like the programmes. His food fads and monumental binges had also become legendary as his girth ballooned to ugly proportions. But it was the drugs that killed him.

Elvis took drugs to wake up, to sleep, to go to the toilet, to leave the toilet, and to go on stage. The results were obvious to all but his most devoted fans;

End of a legend ... overweight Elvis in concert.

he was incoherent and often forgot the words to the songs that had made him famous.

A Baltimore theatre manager recalled: "At one point he dropped his mike and a bodyguard came on stage with another which he held while Presley played his guitar for 20 minutes. The fans began booing because they wanted to hear him sing, not play. Eventually he collapsed and was carried into his dressing room. His bodyguards allowed no one in except his doctor with his medical bag. Thirty minutes later Presley went back on stage totally refreshed."

Elvis was on a roller-coaster ride to destruction. When he died there were a total of thirteen drugs in his bloodstream.

For 22 years, ever since 1956, Elvis had been The King. That year he released *Heartbreak Hotel, Hound Dog, Don't Be Cruel, Blue Suede Shoes* and *Love Me Tender.* The latter was also the title of his first movie. And was the year that Elvis's first appearances on coast-to-coast television turned him into a national entertainment sensation. In 1957 he bought Graceland, a former Memphis church, upon which he lavished his wealth. He also spent it unstintingly on his mother Gladys, whom he adored obsessionally.

When Gladys died at the age of 46, Elvis was distraught with grief. Recalled from military service in the US Army to be with her as she sank into a coma from acute hepatitis and liver failure, Elvis rushed to the hospital in disbelief. Through the night-time silence the wild and despairing wails of Elvis and Gladys's husband Vernon could be heard as they wept over her body. At her funeral Elvis collapsed several times and said: "Oh God, everything I have is gone. Goodbye darling, goodbye, goodbye."

It was a trauma from which he was never to recover. In his office at Graceland he kept to the end a lighted, fully decorated, artificial Christmas tree, a souvenir of the last Christmas they spent together as a family. Albert Goldman, author of one of the hundreds of Presley biographies, said: "Elvis's obsession with his mother lasted throughout his life. It was an unnatural obsession that stretched beyond any normal mother-son bond and certainly accounts for many of Elvis's later sexual problems."

Presley returned to the Army, serving out his term in Germany, where he started popping mild pills – and where he began to display his first real, adult sexual awareness. He had several girlfriends, and on one period of leave in Paris in 1959 he entertained many of the chorus line of the famous Lido nightclub. However, he had found one girl he could lavish true love on: Priscilla Ann Beaulieu, the fourteen-year-old daughter of an army officer. They met at a party in Germany in 1959 and he fell in love with the under-aged beauty. Elvis persuaded his 'Cilla' to dye her hair black, because he liked actress Debra Paget's hair in his 1956 movie *Love Me Tender*.

By now out of the US Army, Elvis invited Priscilla to Graceland for Christmas 1960. After she had returned to Germany, Elvis realised he missed her desperately and called her stepfather, urging him to allow her to finish her schooling in Memphis, under his watchful eye. A year later he relented and Priscilla moved into Graceland in October 1962, although they were not to wed for a further five years. On Priscilla's graduation day from the Immaculate Conception High School, he presented her with a Corvair sports car.

Elvis himself shared his time between the Memphis mansion and Hollywood, where he made 21 movies between 1961 and 1968. Hollywood was also where, unbeknown to Priscilla, he indulged his obsession for small, virginal and often under-aged girls. There might be 50 girls to 8 men at the Californian court of the Hillbilly King, but none of the guys was entitled to a girl until Elvis had taken what he called 'the pick of the litter'.

Hollywood eventually palled as the films he made increasingly flopped. He turned more and more to pills – and to a degree needed them, as he was a chronic insomniac. He was stretching himself to the limit at this time, driving across the country for 24 hours at a stretch, partying and leching with a vengeance. The pills kept him going. He was taking stimulants, tranquillisers, painkillers and Quaaludes, known in Hollywood as the love drug because they improve fading sexual performance. The pills also dulled the disappointment of Elvis's movie and musical failures. His records no longer hit Number One.

Elvis Presley married his Priscilla, now 21 years of

age, on 1 May 1967. They wed in a private suite at the Aladdin Hotel, Las Vegas, and honeymooned in Palm Springs. Nine months later, daughter Lisa Marie was born.

While his wife and daughter stayed at the Presleys' Californian home in Bel Air, Elvis himself spent more and more time on the road. His concert performances seemed to be improving and the money was rolling in again. But there was price to pay, as bodyguard Rick Stanley related: "He didn't show moderation – not just with drugs but with anything he did. When he started getting into needles in 1972 I really began to worry. He was becoming a needlehead. His body began to look like a pincushion."

Presley needed amphetamines to boost his energy for his concerts and he needed uppers to kill his appetite. He would be injected before going on stage and again when he came off. The drugs took a toll of his mental health. His lifestyle became more bizarre and extravagant. In the years before his death he bought four planes. On a tour round Memphis one night he bought fourteen Cadillacs and immediately gave one away to a passing stranger. A few months before his death Elvis was waiting outside his home when he spotted a woman who resembled his beloved mother. Elvis was convinced that she was Gladys Presley reincarnated; he gave her an eighteen-carat gold ring that had been a gift from him to his mother.

Elvis's womanising was equally extravagant. He regularly had his bodyguards pick a young girl from the audience after his show. She would be allowed to meet him only if she agreed to stay the night with the idol.

On one occasion, Elvis almost killed himself and a girl fan, Page Peterson, with drugs. She was eighteen when the star spotted her with her mother at a Las Vegas concert. As he sung his last number, *I Can't Help Falling In Love With You*, he could not take his eyes off her. Said Page later: "A couple of minutes after the curtain came down, when everyone was still cheering, one of Elvis's helpers came up to me and asked if I wanted to meet him. I was taken to his dressing room where he talked about God and politics. He got my mother and me a hotel room but I stayed with Elvis."

Elvis sent for Page on other occasions. On one visit to him in Palm Springs, she complained of a headache and Elvis gave her some pills. She remembered nothing else. Bodyguard Sonny West heard sounds of giggling and slurred words coming from the master-bedroom at 4 o'clock in the morning. That was not unusual. But the following afternoon aides found the couple unconscious in the bedroom – naked and barely breathing. An ambulance took them to hospital where both had their stomachs pumped out.

"I remember the doctor being angry at all the drugs that were in me," said Page. Elvis called my mother and a plane was sent to pick her up. I was in intensive care for two weeks. Later Elvis told me he had paid $10,000 in bribes to hush the whole thing up. He didn't come to see me because he said he would have been recognised. He did send me a verse from the Bible, though. And he did pay all the bills."

It was not the only time that Presley was admitted to hospital. He was taken to Memphis's Baptist Memorial Hospital, officially for hypertension and headaches, but in fact to be dried out. As his old friend Gerry Shering said later: "There were doctors in the town and all over the States who could not say no to him." His drying-out came just nine days after his divorce from Priscilla ...

In 1972 Priscilla had walked out on Presley, whom he sued for divorce on the grounds of her adultery. It was granted on 18 August 1973, and another beauty quickly moved into Graceland: twenty-year-old 'Miss Tennessee' Linda Thompson. But despite being deluged with an avalanche of Cadillacs, jewels, even houses for her and her parents, she too told Elvis in 1976 that she was leaving him.

Linda was followed within months by another Miss Tennessee contestant, this time a runner-up, Ginger Alden. She claimed that they were engaged to be married on Christmas Day 1977. Tragically, Elvis's body rebelled before that date.

Elvis Presley now hid himself from the world, surrounded by his so-called Memphis Mafia of long-time buddies and bodyguards. He was buying $4,000 of pills at a time. He had a liver infection, an enlarged colon and had to wear diapers to go to bed.

The King held court in his bedchamber with walls of button-tufted black suede. The bed was double-king size. In the past it had been used for many a romp but by now he was impotent. In his clothes cupboard was a well-stocked fridge from which he gorged himself on ice-cream. Above it hung the $5,000 sequined jumpsuit into which he could no longer zip himself.

He brightened his life by watching members of the Memphis Mafia having sex with girls in the next-door bedroom, through two-way mirrors he had installed for the purpose. Beside his own bed were a large photograph of his mother, a picture of Jesus Christ and a well-thumbed Bible.

In the early hours of 16 August 1977 Elvis and Ginger Alden returned to Graceland after a late-night visit to the dentist. Elvis had two fillings, while Ginger had only X-rays taken. Between 2.30am and 4.30am Elvis played racquetball and at 6.30am he finally retired to bed with Ginger. The topsy-turvey timetable was thus far not unusual for the star who lived by night and slept by day.

At 9am Ginger awoke to find Elvis also awake. "I'm going into the bathroom to read," he told her.

"Don't fall asleep," said Ginger.

"OK, I won't," he replied.

They were the last words Elvis spoke. More than five hours later, at 2.20pm, Ginger again woke. She sauntered through to the bathroom where she found her lover crumpled on the thickly carpeted floor. He was rushed the short distance to the Baptist Memorial Hospital where he was pronounced dead.

The Memphis state medical examiner, Dr Jerry Francisco, stated that the cause of death was cardiac arrhythmia (an erratic heartbeat). He continued:

"There was severe cardiovascular disease present. He had a history of mild hypertension and some coronary artery disease. Basically it was a natural death."

Not one mention of the killer drug cocktail which must have caused that erratic heartbeat. Yet, as Memphis Mafia member Red West had written just days before Elvis's death: "He takes every possible pill you can think of. He takes pills and shots for downs. He takes a very strong pain medication that is intended for terminally ill cancer patients. He takes pills that he thinks will prevent body odour. He takes pills that he thinks will give him a suntan."

Ginger Alden said she tried to stop Elvis taking drugs. She saw him take a vast pile of them on the night before he died. He told her simply: "I need them."

In 1979 Dr George Nichopolous, Elvis's personal physician, was charged with malpractice. Tennessee public health inspector Steve Belsky said in testimony: "From my experience, Elvis Presley was issued more scheduled uppers, downers and amphetamines than any other individual I have ever seen."

It was revealed that, between January and August 1977, kindly 'Dr Nick' had prescribed to Presley 5,684 narcotic and amphetamine pills, an average of 25 a day. He was suspended from practising for three months, charged with over-prescribing to ten patients, including Elvis and Jerry Lee Lewis. He was later acquitted by a jury and walked free.

DINGO BABY

For a mother to see her baby snatched away in the jaws of a wild dog is horrifying enough. To know of the child's death, ripped apart by snarling, starving animals is the stuff of which nightmares are made. But then to have to suffer the accusations of a court in the most sensational scandal that ever gripped a nation was the final, terrible trauma for Lindy Chamberlain.

The drama that ended in years of legal wrangling and courtroom heartache began on 17 August 1980 in the heart of Australia's Outback. There at sunset, under the mystical shadow of the natural monument, Ayers Rock, the Chamberlain family had struck camp for the night. As well as Lindy, there was her Seventh Day Adventist preacher husband, Michael, and their three children, Aidan, Reagan and baby Azaria. They had all just finished off a barbecue picnic and were preparing to settle down for the night. Nearby was a sign warning: 'DINGOES ARE WILD'.

What occurred next has been the subject of endless speculation and the source of sensational scandal ...

As Michael lingered round the barbecue, Lindy strolled towards their tent to check on nine-week-old Azaria, who had been left in her cot alongside her elder brother Reagan. As she approached the tent, Lindy saw the crouched form of a dingo coming out. As it emerged through the tent flaps, it was shaking its head from side to side. In the darkness she could

Lindy Chamberlain with the baby last seen in a
dingo's jaws.

not make out what was in the dingo's mouth.

Lindy Chamberlain raced into the tent and found Reagan sleeping peacefully but Azaria's cot empty. She searched the tent, sleeping bags, camping equipment, then the scrubland immediately outside. Of little Azaria there was no sign.

Lindy alerted the campsite with her screams: "A dingo has got my baby!"

Despite intensive searches that night and over the ensuing weeks, no body was found, although another visitor did come across some of her clothing, including a baby-stretch garment. Four months after Azaria's disappearance, an inquest was held at Alice Springs. No blame was apportioned for the baby's presumed death, and the coroner's verdict was that "in the time they went to the campsite and the time Mr Chamberlain was at the barbecue area, the death was caused". A year later, however, Northern Territory police declared themselves dissatisfied with the original investigation and they reopened the case.

In 1981 the Chamberlains were called to present their story before a second inquest. They heard police say they were puzzled by the fact that no remains of little Azaria had ever been found, despite the discovery of some of her clothes. Then came the bombshell: Azaria, it was suggested, had been decapitated – the 'proof' being in a blood-stain found on the clothes. It was a woman's handprint, said the police, and meant that Lindy Chamberlain had held the garment while her hands were dripping with blood. There was also blood in their car and in the

Chamberlains' camera bag.

With a growing sense of horror and disgust, Lindy Chamberlain heard the suggestion made that she may have cut off her own baby's head with a pair of scissors.

Suddenly the journalists reporting this minor case in the remote Northern Territory of Australia realised that they had in their notebooks one of the most sensational crime scandals in history. The news was flashed around the world that 33-year-old Lindy was being accused of inventing the entire dingo-snatch story to disguise the grisly murder of her child. The coroner agreed, and the distraught mother was charged with murder, while her husband was charged with being an accessory.

The Chamberlains' seven-week trial was opened in September 1982 in the Northern Territory capital, Darwin. Expert witnesses gave evidence that Azaria's throat had been cut while the child was in the family car. The incision to the jugular had been made while her mother was holding her head. Her garments had then been scattered at Ayers Rock. The entire dingo story was, according to the prosecution, no more than 'a fanciful lie'.

The seven-week trial put the legal bill in the so-called Dingo Baby Case up to $15 million. Lindy sat through it all strangely dispassionate, despite being pregnant with her fourth child. She even showed no emotion when she and Michael were found guilty. Michael was given an eighteen-month suspended sentence. But the judge told Lindy: "You have been found guilty of murder and there is only one sentence I can pass upon you with the law of this territory and that is imprisonment with hard labour for life."

There was an immediate appeal, and Lindy was freed on bail just two days after giving birth to a girl, Kahlia, in prison. Her freedom was short-lived, however. By April 1983 she was back in prison in Darwin, having lost her appeal, just as she did with a subsequent appeal the following year.

Lindy looked set to spend much of her life behind bars. Then came an astonishing change of fortune for the 'murderous' mother. In February 1986 climbers found Azaria's missing matinee jacket in a crevice high on Ayers Rock – in a spot so inaccessible that no ordinary person could have put it there. It could only have been placed there by a climber ... or by a dingo.

Lindy Chamberlain was freed from prison and immediately began the long struggle to clear her name. A judicial inquiry into the case began in October 1986 and did not adjudicate until June the following year. Even then, the conclusion was that there had been insufficient evidence to convict. Lindy was only given a pardon after further machinations by her lawyers, funded at vast expense by their Seventh Day Adventist Church.

The Chamberlains infuriated the Australian legal hierarchy of the time. Lindy Chamberlain announced: "There is no satisfaction in getting a pardon for something you didn't do in the first place. I want the conviction quashed and the authorities to admit that I was wrongly accused." In another outburst, she said: "I don't like your form of law and I don't adhere to it. It's the reason for these courts in Australia being in such a mess."

It took the Chamberlains until 1988 to see justice done. On 15 September, in the Northern Territory Court of Criminal Appeal, Lindy slumped forward in her seat as she heard Chief Justice Austin Asche announce: "We find the original trial is now attended with sufficient doubt to justify this court in quashing the convictions. Not to do so would be unfair and allow an unacceptable risk of perpetuating a miscarriage of justice."

Lindy said: "I always knew some time it would come right. I just didn't know when. If you let your self-esteem go, if you lose your self-respect, you lose your grip on everything else. I didn't. I fight first."

The Chamberlains had won their fight to clear their names but they still sought compensation from their accusers. They were aided by the publicity caused by Lindy's book, *Through My Eyes*, and by a movie, *Cry In The Dark*, starring Meryl Streep. Eventually the Northern Territory government granted the Chamberlains a total of about $7 million in compensation. They did not feel it was half enough for their wrecked lives and for the suspicions that still haunt them.

As Lindy said: "Some people will die believing we are guilty. We just have to live with that."

ROBERTO CALVI

The prestigious Banco Ambrosiano, of Milan, is sometimes known as 'The Priests' Bank' because of its hundred-year connection with its founding fathers within the Catholic hierarchy. In the Seventies its chairman was Roberto Calvi, seemingly staid, certainly profit-conscious, who was known by some as 'God's Banker' because he handled a large proportion of the Vatican's vast investments.

Calvi's task was to make as much money as possible for the Vatican in particular, and several other investors in general, in fierce competition with the commercial banks of Italy. To a certain extent, these rivals banks were expected to play tough and dirty in the money markets. Banco Ambrosiano, by contrast, was expected to be as near to godly as possible. To make his mark, however, Roberto Calvi employed whatever means he could – despite representing the interests of the Holy Father.

Calvi laundered 'hot money' and ran phoney companies. His less-than-reputable business clients required respectability, and his Vatican clients needed their assets worth billions moved into areas where much-needed income could be created. Calvi made the two sides – God and mammon – work unwittingly together.

In 1978 Calvi's handling of criminally-tainted accounts drew the attention of the nation's controlling body, the Bank of Italy, towards the

Banker Roberto Calvi: found hanged under a London bridge.

Banco Ambrosiano. Calvi asked one of his clients, businessman Licio Gelli, to 'influence' investigators not to probe too deeply.

But there was reason beyond business acquaintanceship why Gelli stepped in successfully to help Calvi. Some time before, Gelli had enlisted the banker in the secret society of Freemasonry. Calvi had joined Rome's right-wing Freemason's Lodge P2, of which Gelli was Grand Master, controlling a network of fellow members in every strata of the business community, the military, the police, the judiciary and the government.

The connections Calvi made within Lodge P2 were invaluable. They were also highly dangerous ...

In March 1981 investigators probing Sicilian-American business dealings raided Gelli's home. The businessman had flitted to South America but several of the documents he had left behind made clear the involvement of influential Lodge P2 members, including Roberto Calvi.

In a Milan prison cell, Calvi 'sang'. He gave chapter and verse of the secret dealings between the Vatican and the Freemasons. As a reward, he was sentenced to four years in jail for currency swindles – but was freed on appeal and welcomed back to his old job.

Calvi's principal contact at the Vatican was Archbishop Paul Marcinkus, a burly Chicago-born bodyguard who ran the Vatican's internal bank and whose motto was: "You can't run a Church on Hail Marys alone."

Marcinkus had issued 'letters of comfort' to Calvi guaranteeing some of the foreign companies he had set up to launder money. But Calvi's foreign currency dealings were anything up to $2,000 million adrift. Eventually Marcinkus ran out of patience with his Banco Ambrosiano friend and called in the debts.

In May 1982 Calvi flew in to London's Heathrow Airport on a false passport, warning friends:

"A lot of people have a lot to answer for. If the whole thing comes out it will be enough to start World War III."

For three weeks, the diminutive, 62-year-old banker hid away in a flat in Chelsea, rented under an assumed name. It was believed that he was attempting to contact Freemasonry friends in England who could help him find a new identity abroad.

On 17 June he suddenly disappeared from his apartment. The following morning he was found hanging under Blackfriars Bridge in the City of London, his body weighted down with bricks.

An inquest decided that Calvi had committed suicide. Then doubts were raised and a reconvened hearing decided that an 'open verdict' would be a safer conclusion, since no one knew who had taken the banker's life.

The answer, however, was easier to discern for those in the Freemason's movement back in Rome. Calvi had broken his word by informing on fellow members. It was clear to them why he had been found beneath the bridge of the 'Black Friars', with its ancient religious connotations, and why he had been suspended with the ebb and flow of the Thames tides washing around his feet. Lodge P2 colleagues recalled the ritual oath of loyalty he had made when he guaranteed his lifelong protection of his lodge brothers. Breaking that oath would earn Calvi a ritual murder ...

"Having my tongue torn out and being buried in the sand at low water's mark, or a cable length from the shore where the tide ebbs and flows."

DIANE JONES

The quaint old village of Coggeshall in the Essex countryside could have leapt straight from the pages of an Agatha Christie thriller – and the scandal that bubbled behind the lace curtains of this English beauty spot was one that the mistress of mystery would herself have been proud of.

The stories that shocked sleepy Coggeshall poured out after the disappearance of the wife of the village doctor. During the three months that the hunt for her was pursued, the place became a mecca for news-hungry reporters speculating about the missing woman and digging into her and her husband's past lives. There was an eruption of scandalous stories that slipped behind the mask of respectability the village had assumed. Masked that is until the night of 23 July 1983 when Diane Jones had too much to drink in the local pub, The Woolpack ...

Diane Jones, aged 35 at the time, was the third wife of doctor Robert Jones. The doctor, then aged 40, often stayed late in The Woolpack with Diane, who was known in the village as a rather eccentric woman who drank too much. The pub was one of the few places where the doctor was seen regularly with his wife, talking with friends, sharing a drink with the landlord, relaxing in the saloon bar. The marriage was not happy; 'stormy' was the word most used by locals to describe it. Diane had been one of the doctor's patients and the couple had first met when he was treating her for depression. They were married in 1982. The first hint that all was not well with the relationship was when Dr Jones arrived to take his surgery one morning with two black eyes.

It transpired that he had been involved in a fight with one of Diane's ex-lovers, a swimming pool attendant called Paul Barnes. Not long after this episode, Diane was charged with dangerous driving – she had driven the wrong way down the A12 dual carriageway close to the home she shared with Dr Jones – and also with stealing a bottle of champagne from a hotel.

After the court case, Diane told reporters that her husband repeatedly threw her out of the house and that he had punched her. Dr Jones replied to this accusation: "Diane used to go on these benders and smash the place up. I had to use violence to restrain her."

Their marriage was clearly turbulent, and the state of their relationship was now public knowledge. Their baby daughter was taken into care because the social services considered that the marital home was not a safe place for the child to be.

On the last night Diane was seen alive she was drinking heavily in The Woolpack. The inn echoed to her raucous laughter – until her husband ordered her to quieten down. There was a blazing row and the evening ended when she toppled from her bar stool and he carried her out of the pub to take her home. It was the last time Diane Jones was seen alive.

The following day, life, it seemed, went back to

normal. The doctor returned to his surgery, where he was assisted in his work by his receptionist Sue Smith, his ex-wife, who was now remarried to a wealthy antiques dealer, John Smith.

There was no sign of Diane in the village that day. Nor the next, nor the one after that. Nine days passed before Dr Jones reported to the police that his wife had vanished after the drinking binge at The Woolpack. He said he had taken her home, and then she had run off into the night. "She often disappeared before," Dr Jones told police, and said that was the reason why he did not report her absence earlier.

The disappearance, combined with the characterful location and the steamy, stormy marriage, caused the press to swoop on Coggeshall. The tiny streets were choked with the media circus. Newsmen from foreign newspapers and television channels engulfed the village. The Americans in particular lapped up the 'Miss Marple' setting as the hunt for Diane Jones widened and the torrid facts about her marriage began to pour out.

Mrs Jones's ex-lovers stepped forward to tell of their nights of passion with the doctor's wife. Tales of her wild abandon greeted the doctor at his breakfast table each morning with the arrival of the papers. Even his ex-wife Sue Smith was to reveal to a newspaper that it was the doctor's infidelity that led her to divorce him on grounds of adultery.

The police searched the doctor's home and garden but found nothing. The conclusions the press drew were the same as those the villagers had been talking about ever since the disappearance: that Dr Jones was in some way connected with it. He himself stressed both publicly and privately that he had not harmed his wife on the night she vanished. The doctor did admit, however, that his marriage to Diane had reached breaking point around the time she went missing. He said that he was exasperated by her drinking and her lovers. But harm her? Never.

Dr Jones put on a brave face at the suspicion and innuendo levelled at him. He attended his surgery regularly and tried, amidst the publicity, to lead a normal life. But he was never out of the headlines. He was charged with drunk driving just weeks after Diane had vanished, the result of a night he had spent drinking with his old adversary, Paul Barnes.

All through the summer and into the autumn Dr Jones endured the attention of the world's press. Then, three months to the day since her disappearance, and just when it looked as if the enquiry might be about to wind down, a gruesome discovery was made 48 kilometres from Coggeshall, in a wood at Brightwell, Suffolk.

Beaters on a pheasant shoot on 23 October 1989 discovered a hunched-up bundle in their path. It was the badly decomposed body of Diane Jones. She was not the only murder victim. A pathologist revealed that she had been three months pregnant at the time of the murder.

Other forensic clues which detectives had pinned their hopes on were sadly lacking. Vital evidence had been lost because of the time the body had lain undiscovered in the woodland.

The doctor, who had suffered the ignominy of having his garden excavated, his floorboards pulled up and who had endured hours of questioning by detectives, returned from a holiday in Wales when the body was discovered – only to find that police had removed yet more objects and furniture from his house. The police announced publicly that they planned to interview again everyone they had initially questioned about Mrs Jones's disappearance.

Then on 14 November came the most dramatic development of all. In a dawn swoop at three homes, Dr Jones, his ex-wife Sue Smith and Paul Barnes were taken in for questioning. After twelve hours Mrs Smith emerged to say: "I don't know why they took me in for questioning. But it was not an ordeal. It was all very amicable."

Dr Jones, however, was questioned for three days. After he was taken into custody, experts from the Home Office Forensic Laboratory in Huntingdon, Cambridgeshire, arrived at his home. They cordoned off the two-acre garden into ten-metre wide strips with white ribbon. Police officers dug several holes while their colleagues searched the excavated areas with metal detectors. Later the metal gate across the entrance to the drive was dismantled and taken away to police headquarters for further forensic examination.

After Dr Jones's lengthy stay in custody there was speculation that the police were considering making charges against him. But as abruptly as he was arrested, he was freed. He was told to report back to the police early in 1984 when their enquiries had continued further.

Nevertheless, the doctor continued to attract scandal. In October 1984, his girlfriend Gina McFarlane bore him a daughter. This was no simple affair, however. Gina McFarlane was the daughter of Roz McFarlane, who had kept house for the doctor – until she discovered he was having an affair with her daughter.

However, by now Dr Robert Jones was able to enjoy a little more privacy from the press and the police. He had been officially ruled out of the investigation into his wife's death. The hunt for the killer was discontinued, but the case remains open. Just what happened to Diane Jones that night will probably never be known.

PRINCESS MICHAEL
OF KENT

Marie-Christine von Reibnitz, Czech-born but having spent most of her life in Australia, arrived in London in the 'Swinging Sixties' and set about building herself a rich future – and a romantically historic past!

She let it be known that she was a baroness, that her grandmother was 'Her Serene Highness Princess Hedwig-Graetz' and her grandfather had been Australian ambassador to the Czar of Russia in St Petersburg. Before long she had met wealthy young banker and Old Etonian Tom Troubridge and they were married in 1971. She was 26.

A little over a year later Troubridge was posted to Bahrain on business and in time Marie-Christine found herself being pursued by a new suitor. She was heard to cancel an evening engagement with a girlfriend, reputedly giving the excuse: "I have a very big fish on the hook at the moment and I don't want to let him off."

Prince Michael of Kent, one of the British Royal Family's most eligible bachelors, had fallen in love with Marie-Christine while she was still married to his friend Troubridge. Worse was that, as their love developed and they laid plans for Marie-Christine's divorce and remarriage, she was a Catholic and Prince Michael was at the very heart of the Establishment of

Princess Michael of Kent: Her father was a Nazi officer.

the Church of England, of which the Queen is head.

In 1977 Marie-Christine applied to the Roman Catholic Church to annul her marriage. She also filed for a civil divorce. The latter was granted in April 1978 and a week later the Queen gave permission for her and Prince Michael to wed. However, the Queen stipulated that Michael must renounce his right of succession to the throne, that he must guarantee that any children would be raised as Anglicans and not Roman Catholics, and thirdly that they must marry abroad.

Meanwhile, the Pope had refused to annul the Troubridge marriage. Humiliatingly for the haughty Marie-Christine, this meant that she and Michael were forced to make do with a civil marriage in Vienna town hall.

Prince Michael and his new bride settled down to live in royal apartments at Kensington Palace. They also bought a country home in Gloucestershire. Michael quit the Army and sought directorships of companies in the City of London. After a year of marriage, a son was born; a daughter followed eighteen months later.

The princess's mother, Marianne, continued to live in Australia. Her divorced father, Gunther, who had emigrated to Mozambique after World War II, died there at the age of 89. But apart from that one tinge of sadness, the couple seemed deliriously happy, the Prince obviously and utterly devoted to his beautiful blonde wife.

Then the careful image that the refugee princess

had cultivated over the years began to crumble. The institution of the British Royal Family was to be seen at its flimsiest. It was as if a corner of the royal red carpet had been turned up and the cleaner had been caught out sweeping the dirt beneath it. The time bomb ticking away beneath the Royal Family finally exploded on Monday 15 April 1985 when a reporter phoned the palace and gently but firmly inquired whether it was true that Princess Michael's father, at that time supposedly one of the Second World War's innocent sufferers, had in fact been a major in the reviled SS.

The Buckingham Palace press office tried to contact Princess Michael but she was out for the afternoon. They left a message for her. The princess returned to her apartments at Kensington Palace at 6pm and opened the envelope containing the deferential inquiry. According to press reports at the time, the princess simply panicked. She said it was "a wicked lie" and she would do anything to prevent its publication.

Her aides attempted to calm her as she threatened injunctions and writs. They implored her to check the story out with her mother before making any response to the press. A phone call was put through to her mother in Australia and, as she listened to the old lady's hesitant answers, she realised that the awful truth would have to be revealed to the world. On the advice of the palace, the princess agreed to issue a terse official statement:

"Princess Michael confirmed tonight that it is true

that her father was a member of the SS. It came as a total surprise to her when she heard the news. There will be no further comment or statement from the princess."

The scandal made the front page of half the newspapers of the Western world. Members of both British and European parliaments demanded inquiries. In New York, Jewish militants decried the 'royal cover-up'. Within days, Princess Michael had to break her earlier vow of silence and, as allegations of a cover-up grew ever stronger, took the unprecedented step of going on nationwide television in a bid to curtail the controversy. Her appearance was excruciatingly embarrassing, not only for her but for the entire Royal Family.

Under obvious strain, Princess Michael admitted to viewers that she had known about her father's membership of the Nazi party but not of his membership of the SS. She said:

"It is a deep shame for me. I think it was sufficiently shocking that he had been in the Nazi party but I did not think to look further. It came as a very great blow to me because I always rather hero-worshipped him. When told this report was coming out, I immediately telephoned by mother and said 'Guess what they are trying to pin on me now.' And she said, 'But I'm afraid it is true.' I have been in a sort of state of shell-shock ever since but it is some-thing I'll have to come to terms with, and I know that I shall. I don't like it but I have to live with it."

Princess Michael could have stopped there. She

would have been wise to have done so but she then spoke of a document which, she claimed, "actually exonerates my father; which states quite clearly that his position in the SS was an honorary one". She added: "I was brought up to believe that the SS meant one thing – concentration camps for Jews and so on. I have now discovered that he was not involved in anything like that at all."

Inevitably, such an obvious attempt to excuse her father's past was bound to add fuel to the flames. It certainly fuelled the public's demand for further details of her family's sensational history. Incredibly, these details were not hard to find. While reporters from the national press rushed to London's Heathrow Airport en route to Germany and Austria to hunt down obscure relatives and even more obscure archives, it was discovered that the facts about Baron von Reibnitz had been readily available for years. They were to be found in dusty archives just three miles from Buckingham Palace, in official lists of senior SS officers which had been held in the Imperial War Museum since the early sixties.

Von Reibnitz's military history soon became as well known as that of most members of the British Royal Family. Born on 8 September 1894, he had won an Iron Cross (second-class) and a Front Line Soldiers' Cross in the First World War. In 1935 his military rank was that of Untersturmfuhrer (equivalent to the rank of a British second-lieutenant).

By October 1944 he had risen to the rank of Sturmbannfuhrer (major). Most sinisterly, one of the honours bestowed on him was the SS 'Death Head' ring. Documents turned up by reporters even revealed a letter from von Reibnitz to Adolf Hitler, asking permission to marry the Countess Marianne Szapary. In the letter he says: "I was used as a political speaker in the years of the struggle."

Perhaps most telling was von Reibnitz's Nazi party number: 412855. It revealed the very early stage at which he had joined. Veteran Nazi hunter Simon Wiesenthal said: "This means that he pledged his loyalty to Hitler and the Hitler ideals and hatreds in the early 1920s."

It is clear that von Reibnitz's Nazi role was lengthy and active. It was even suggested that he may have been planted as a Hitler spy in the early street-fighting stormtroopers, the SA. He switched to the SS at the age of 39, shortly before Hitler wiped out the SA. Von Reibnitz was promoted just four days after the bloodbath.

It is not likely that von Reibnitz took part in any of the more horrific excesses of the SS. As a captain, he saw action in Poland. But in 1944 he rejoined the Roman Catholic Church. This was judged a 'character weakness' by the SS and he was forced to resign.

With daily banner headlines such as 'This Bloody Disgrace' shaming the Royal Family around the world, Princess Michael used her influence to employ the British Ambassador in Bonn, Sir Julian Bullard, in a search for documents that might clear her father. He quickly came up with the findings of tribunals to which he had applied under the post-war Nazi 'declassification' programme. Sadly for the princess, they rejected his petition seeking total exoneration, although its moderate findings went far towards defusing the immediate scandal.

However, it did not ameliorate the long-term damage done to the institution of the British monarchy. Far from it. Princess Michael had made her new relatives a laughing stock. Few royal-watchers doubted that she had been heavily vetted by Scotland Yard or even M15 long before her marriage, yet the secret of her father's past had been ignored, or worse, covered up.

So far, Princess Michael's handling of the scandal had done little to endear her to the rest of the Royal Family, who scathingly referred to her as 'Princess Pushy'. Nor was she the general public's favourite royal. Now, however, where denials had failed, tears won ...

Under obvious strain, the princess made a rare speech at an official function. She spoke sadly of her ordeal, hesitated, then her voice broke and she was reduced to tears. The effect of her public sorrow gained her public sympathy. The scandal began to be yesterday's news. Princess Pushy had at last succeeded in pushing it under the carpet!

BILL CLINTON

The whiff of scandal is nothing new at the White House. Every president in recent times has run the gauntlet of rumour and innuendo.

But no First Citizen has ever received a baptism of fire comparable to the early months of Bill Clinton's administration. Whatever the truth about the charges of financial and sexual misbehaviour, one thing is sure. The mud has already stuck.

Clinton's first year following the November 1992 election victory was a shambolic mess. His young, inexperienced White House staff managed to clog up the machinery of state with long and rambling policy meetings. Older and wiser heads in Washington began to grumble about what they called 'Clinton Standard Time', a reference to the inability of the President's managers to get him to stick to his schedules.

Even the chain of command itself began to go fuzzy. It was difficult enough for administrators to handle Hillary Clinton's role as unofficial president in charge of reforming health care. They also had to handle a president who wanted personal control over everything, a recipe for organisational anarchy in a nation as big as the US.

It was just this background that produced the humiliation in Somalia. The Defence Department tried to feel its way through the crisis unsure what the State Department was doing. The State Department, in any case, didn't know what the White House was

Gennifer Flowers ... scandalous tales about President Clinton.

doing. All three offices spent their time trying to get vital decisions out of the president while his mind was focused on a master-plan for health care reforms. In the end Secretary of State Warren Christopher demanded a clear one hour per week from Clinton to try to break the log-jam.

All this could have been forgiven the new president. But the persistent allegations of his appetite for adulterous sex, coupled with the so-called Whitewatergate land deals scandal, gave American electors the impression that here was a White House sinking ever-deeper into a mire of its own making.

The charge that Clinton was an adulterer had been pressed home even before he became President. A blonde cabaret singer, 43-year-old Gennifer Flowers, told how he liked her to place dollops of apple pie and whipped cream at strategic points on her naked body before gobbling up the gooey mess. She also claimed that during their twelve-year affair he liked her to dress up for sex in a cheerleader's outfit or in stockings and high heels. He was, she insisted, not very well endowed but 'very accommodating with his tongue'.

Gennifer said she first made love to Clinton in 1977 when he was Arkansas attorney-general. They had sex up to four times a night. Once, state troopers were said to have stood guard outside a room in the governor's mansion while their boss and Gennifer copulated on a kitchen table.

On another occasion the guard was posted outside the men's room while the couple were making love

White House laywer Vincent Foster was found shot in a park.

inside. At the time, Hillary was standing only a few yards away.

Gennifer says she has a collection of taped conversations proving she is telling the truth. In one, a man she claims is Clinton tells her never to admit their relationship if confronted by the media. "If they ever hit you with it just say no," he says. "There's nothing they can do."

Clinton might have been able to ride out the shock waves from Gennifer's kiss'n'tell account. He certainly impressed many voters when he and Hilary went on the *60 Minutes* television show together a few months before the election.

Clinton categorically denied any affair with Gennifer but did admit to unspecified 'wrong-doing' and 'causing pain in my marriage'. His tearful confession, in which he pledged his future whole-heartedly to Hillary, seemed to satisfy many voters.

OK, the guy had gone astray but now he was back in the fold. He'd been honest enough to tell the nation.

That could have been the end of the matter but for the accounts of two Arkansas state cops who had been Clinton's bodyguards and part-time batmen during the thirteen years he was governor. Their accounts of his sexual misdemeanours were both damning and detailed. Now, even the usually unquestioning heavyweight American newspapers began to sit up and take notice. Both *The Los Angeles Times* and *The American Spectator* led the pack.

In all, four Arkansas troopers levelled accusations

against the President. Two of them were prepared to be named – Larry Patterson, 43, and Roger Perry, 47 – and their accounts were nothing short of dynamite. They told how they had been expected to fix up girls who caught the governor's eye, arrange clandestine meetings between him and his mistresses and, above all, make sure Hillary stayed in the dark.

The officers, who between them had 43 years service, worked for Clinton between 1979 and 1993. They insisted they had no complaints against him as a boss and liked the way his personality mixed intelligence, quick wit and country crudeness.

Clinton would make them laugh with antics such as eating his baked potatoes in two bites or cracking cynical jokes about his job. One of his favourite quips was: "I gotta stay in politics because I'm too old to be a movie star."

So far the Clinton scandals had turned out to be titilating and embarrassing, but hardly the stuff of impeachment. It was only when some newspapers began hinting at an attempted cover-up – a vice the US media will never permit its presidents – that the saga took a new and sinister twist.

First came the disappearance of two videos, allegedly containing damaging footage of Clinton in pursuit of sexual favours. One, shot by an unidentified lawyer, was said to show the President standing at the front door of Gennifer's home. The lawyer claimed he lived next door to her at the time.

He said the tape was stolen by three hoodlums who smashed their way into his house in June 1992 and beat him up. "I want to know who was behind the incident," he told one newspaper. "You cannot help but wonder."

The second video was shot by trooper Larry Patterson, who says it showed Clinton in the front of a pick-up truck with a perfume shop girl. He says he got a clear view of the President having sex with her as he aimed the remote-controlled security camera mounted on top of a 30ft pole. The whole scene was projected down to a 27-inch screen in the guards' house.

Patterson said: "He was sitting on the passenger side and she was behind the wheel. I pointed the thing directly into the windshield and watched on the screen as the governor received oral sex." This video later disappeared. Patterson claimed that any incriminating material, including logs at the security gate, were destroyed on Hillary Clinton's orders after her husband won the presidency.

The role Patterson and Perry played in undermining Clinton took an intriguing new twist in early September 1993 as The *American Spectator* magazine prepared to publish its stories. In a bizarre echo of Richard Nixon's Watergate scandal, the offices of The *Spectator* in Washington were burgled twice in the space of a week.

Each time the raiders carried out the laborious task of cutting through the walls of adjoining offices, and each time files were searched. After all that trouble, the only items stolen were a personal stereo, a portable radio, a fax machine and a video recorder.

Four days later the magazine's New York suite was also burgled and drawers searched. Nothing was taken.

The portrayal of the President as a philanderer was only just beginning. A few months later, preacher's daughter Paula Corbin-Jones announced she was filing a lawsuit alleging that Clinton made 'unwelcome sexual advances' to her in a hotel room and then asked her to perform a sex act. When she refused, he allegedly became reproachful and left her fearing for her career. He mentioned that he knew her employer well.

The incident was said to have occurred in 1991 while Clinton was still the Arkansas governor. One of his bodyguards approached Paula in the foyer of the state's Excelsior Hotel and asked if she'd like to meet Clinton in an upstairs room. She agreed, believing he wanted to discuss her job prospects (she was then working as a conference receptionist).

By the end of 1993 the spotlight was turning onto yet another aspect of the Clintons' personal lives, their dealings with an Arkansas land company called Whitewater Development.

This was the most complicated of the potential scandals facing the President ... and also the most serious. The Clintons had been partners in the risky company with one James McDougal, owner of the Madison Guaranty bank which had gone bust in 1989.

Federal investigators soon started taking a keen interest in whether cash from the floundering bank made its way to the Clinton Presidential Campaign Fund. They also wanted to know if the governor actively shielded McDougal's activities from state regulators, who had been worried for years about the solvency status of the bank.

The implications got worse. In July 1993 a key White House lawyer, Vincent Foster, 48, was found dead in the heavily-wooded and secluded Fort Marcy park on the outskirts of Washington. In his right hand was a Colt .38 revolver with his forefinger still round the trigger. There was one round left in the gun and a bullet casing nearby. Foster appeared to have killed himself with a single shot fired upwards into his brain.

The reaction from the Clintons was, in every respect, both human and genuine. They were devastated by the loss of their personal lawyer and friend, a man who had known Bill Clinton since their high school days back in Arkansas. He had given Hillary her break as a lawyer with the prestigious Rose firm in Little Rock. He was her confidant and mentor, the man who had helped her through her marriage problems in the mid-eighties and who was now, some whispered, her secret lover.

"It is an immense personal loss to me and to Hillary," Clinton said the day after the body was found. "There is no way to know how these things happen." The President said he knew his friend had been feeling depressed but had no idea that he was on the verge of despair.

So was it a straightforward suicide? Of all the traumas of Clinton's first years in office, Vincent

Foster's death is undoubtably the strangest.

For a start, ambulancemen who retrieved the body were struck by how straight it was lying – "almost as though it was in a coffin," one said later. There was no gunpowder around the wound or on Foster's tongue, no traces of blood on the barrel and no damaged teeth. Oddly, the gun had remained in the dead man's hand. Normally the recoil of a self-inflicted shot to the brain sends the weapon spinning wildly from the scene.

Within four hours of the discovery of the body, Clinton's chief legal counsel Bernard Nussbaum, together with Patsy Thomasson, a Democratic stalwart from Arkansas, and Margaret Williams, Hillary's chief of staff, began an intensive search of Foster's office. Incredibly it had not been sealed and guarded, as was normal procedure.

Whatever the motives, it is clear that some of the files which were removed over the next two days – against the wishes of the Park Police and the FBI – included details of the Clintons' personal investments in Whitewater.

Did Foster kill himself because he believed he'd let them down? Did he feel he should have sold out their holding long before the media had ever heard the property company's name? Or did someone, for whatever reason, decide to murder him.

History will be the judge. And only time will tell if Bill Clinton's battered reputation will recover.

NANCY KERRIGAN AND TONYA HARDING

The beautiful young skater was laughing and joking with a woman reporter as she made her way off the ice and back to her dressing room in Detroit's Cobo Hall. It was 2.35pm on 6 January 1994 and the end of another demanding practice session. Nancy Kerrigan felt she was as ready as she could be for the opening of the US figure skating championships the following day.

Every competitor knew the stakes. The winner was guaranteed a place in the national Olympic team and the chance of glory the following month at the Lillehammer games. Kerrigan was optimistic, if a little nervous.

Around her a handful of other hopefuls lingered with their coaches and a few photographers. Nancy's parents Dan and Brenda Kerrigan looked on proudly amid the bustle of technicians, rink officials and TV crews. They knew their little girl had worked so hard for this moment.

Suddenly a man dressed in a black hat and black leather jacket broke into a run. Those who watched him move had a split-second to realise that he looked totally out of place before he dashed between Nancy and the reporter, pulled out a 21 inch black retractable baton and whipped it mercilessly across the skater's right knee. The contact was so loud it

Icy encounters ... Nancy Kerrigan and Tonya Harding.

echoed across the ice.

Instantly Nancy crumpled to the floor crying in agony and shouting: "Why me? Why me? Why now? Help me. It hurts so bad. Please help me!" Seconds later her father was at her side, scooping her into his arms and calling for help. As he cradled her she continued to sob: "It hurts, Dad. I'm so scared. Why me? Why now? Why?"

Across the ice her attacker was smashing through a Plexiglass partition to reach a waiting getaway car. He had already discarded a note designed to portray him as a vengeful madman. Now he threw away the metal club as well. He was confident he would not be caught and that Nancy Kerrigan, the 24-year-old golden girl of American skating, would not be troubling the judges at Lillehammer the following month.

In hospital, however, doctors discovered Nancy had not sustained a career-ending injury. The baton had fallen around half an inch too high to cause a break and, although the full extent of the damage was not immediately clear, the signs looked positive. Nancy had escaped with severe bruising on her kneecap and on the quadriceps tendon.

A couple of hours later, and visibly brighter, she told a TV reporter: "I just don't want to lose faith in a lot of people. It was just one bad guy, and I'm sure there's others, but not everyone is like that."

She begged her doctors to let her compete the following day. It was, she told them, her big chance to try for an Olympic gold medal. But by evening Nancy knew in her heart that there was no chance. Her knee had swollen up like a football and she couldn't bend it. Even when surgeons drained twenty cubic centimetres of blood from the affected area it made no difference. When she tried to hop on her right foot she was hopelessly lacking in control. Confronted with the inescapable truth, Nancy broke down and cried.

The following day she sat in Detroit's Joe Louis Arena and watched wordlessly as Tonya Harding took the women's title. Nancy had been hot favourite and millions of Americans shared her anguish. She was their kind of hero: elegant, graceful, attractive (many said she looked like the young Katharine Hepburn) and hugely talented. Harding had given an excellent performance but she couldn't demand the same kind of public adulation. Unlike Nancy's middle-class American upbringing, Tonya was a girl from the wrong side of the tracks. A gum-chewer, smoker, and plain speaker, she showed too much of an ambitious streak for the fans' liking.

Harding had won her ticket for Lillehammer and the second team place looked to be going to the exciting young skater Michelle Kwan. But the United States Figure Skating Association invoked a little-known regulation to give Nancy the place, provided she recovered from her injuries in time.

The next day 22-year-old Tonya and Nancy posed side by side for a photograph of the entire US Olympic team. "Congratulations, you skated great last night," ventured Nancy. "I hope you feel better,"

Harding replied.

It all seemed very amicable. Yet some observers of the ice scene wondered whether, lurking in the background, there might be skulduggery afoot. Hadn't the tennis star Monica Seles been stabbed by a Steffi Graf fan so that she couldn't challenge his idol? Hadn't an over-ambitious Texan mother recently tried to see off her daughter's cheerleading rival by shooting that girl's mother? These were surely thoughts that must have entered Nancy's head as she recuperated with her family at Stoneham, Massachusetts. If so, she gave no public hint.

Back in Detroit the mystery was already beginning to unravel. A woman telephoned police anonymously saying she had heard a tape recording of three men plotting an attack on Kerrigan. She knew all three and she gave their names. The inquiry moved west into Portland, Oregon, Tonya Harding's home town.

Then Gary Crowe, a teacher at the Pioneer Pacific College near Portland, told detectives that one of his students had also heard the tape. It belonged to one Shawn Eric Eckardt, 26, a 350 lb bodyguard to Tonya. Eckardt's voice was on the tape as was Harding's former husband, Jeff Gillooly. Gillooly could be clearly heard saying: "Why don't we just kill her?" Eckardt replied: "We don't need to kill her. Let's just hit her in the leg."

Surveillance of Eckardt soon led to 29-year-old Derrick Smith, the driver of the getaway car, and to Smith's nephew Shane Stant, the 20-year-old weightlifter who struck Kerrigan. They were an inept crew and detectives were left wondering whether there weren't some real brains behind the plot. But initially both Harding and Gillooly denied any involvement. "I have more faith in my wife than to bump off the competition," said Gillooly.

In fact, Gillooly had been obsessed with attacking Kerrigan since well before Christmas. He reckoned that if Tonya could make the Olympic team she would be launched into a star-studded career. Eckhardt had more down-to-earth reasoning. If one ice skater was attacked others would quickly get scared. That had to be good news for his company, which supplied bodyguards to the rich and famous. The men discussed cutting through Nancy's Achilles tendon, or even 'taking her out' with a sniper, but in the end opted for a single strike on her knee.

Harding insisted that she had no prior knowledge of what was going on. After an interview with police on January 18, at which the whole story was unravelled, she announced that she was again separating from Gillooly. Their on-off relationship, which had enjoyed a renaissance towards the end of 1993, was once again in tatters.

The following day Gillooly was charged with conspiracy to commit assault and a full confession soon followed. From his jail cell he then began firing wild accusations at Tonya, claiming that she was in on the plot from the start. According to Gillooly, it was Tonya who made the final decision to attack Nancy. He said she picked him up after a meeting of the conspirators and allegedly told him: "OK. Let's do it."

Tonya again denied involvement. But after hearing of her ex's confession she admitted she had known that the beating of Kerrigan was carried out by "persons close to me". Though she had this information within days of the assault, she agreed she had failed to pass it on to the FBI.

There was a growing feeling among many Americans that whatever the truth behind the sporting scandal, Tonya was tainted and should not go to Lillehammer. But the star herself refused to be cowed. Showing all the fight that had helped her become a stunning skater in her own right, she issued a statement pleading to stay in the Olympic team.

"Despite my mistakes and my rough edges," she said, "I have done nothing to violate the standards of excellence that are expected of an Olympic athlete. I have devoted my entire life to one objective: winning an Olympic gold medal for my country. This is my last chance."

She won her argument. Nancy won her battle to regain fitness. As the games got underway both women stepped on to the ice at Lillehammer for practice. They exchanged neither a word nor a glance but for the watching millions around the world it was a breathtaking piece of real life soap opera.

In the US, particularly, the desire for Nancy to win was overpowering. It would have been the perfect fairy-tale ending. The triumph of courage and determination over dirty tricks. The crowning of a beautiful ice queen. Some TV stations played up this bias against Tonya by repeatedly showing footage of her falling in practice.

America's dream was not to be. As the judges announced their final marks on the evening of February 26th, Nancy found herself in the silver position, pipped to a gold medal by the brilliant young Ukrainian skater Oksana Baiul. Tonya Harding finished eighth.